Della's Destiny

A women's adventure AROUND AUSTRALIA with her horse and dog

Maricy Dalsanto

All rights reserved. No part of this book may be reproduced or transmitted in any form or by any means, electronic or mechanical, including photocopying, recording, or by any information storage and retrieval system, without permission in writing from the publisher.

Published in 2014
by Maricy Dalsanto

Typesetting and design
by Publicious Pty Ltd
www.publicious.com.au

*Catalogue-in-Publication details available
from the National Library of Australia*

ISBN: 978-0-9925879-0-1

Also available in ebook
ebook ISBN: 978-0-9925879-1-8

Copyright © Maricy Dalsanto 2014
Non-fiction — Adventure — Pets — Travel

A portion of the proceeds from the sales of this book will be donated to The Animal Welfare League of Queensland to support the great work they do on behalf of Queensland's homeless and abandoned animals.

For more information, please see www.awlqld.com.au

For Della and Lucky

ACKNOWLEDGEMENTS

This book is dedicated to my faithful and loving dog Della, Lucky and the horses who accompanied me on this adventure. It's for all the people I met along the way - those who gave me advice, assistance, meals and accommodation in their homes and on their property and everyone who helped and offered water and places to camp. Without their help we could not have completed this trip.

My thanks also go to my friends who stopped by, Yasmin Sayer who mailed me packages, Broadbeach 'Old Boys' AFL Club for the horse float, and those who donated to the charity.

Finally, my thanks to Terry Spring, who fashioned my diary into a comprehensive record of my five thousand kilometre trip, Jessica Walker for proof reading and correcting my many mistakes, James Hughes for designing my cover and to Andy McDermott (Publicious) for assisting me to publish this book.

ABOUT THE AUTHOR

Maricy Dalsanto grew up loving animals and the 'great outdoors' in a semi-rural area in a household that had its share of pets. She travelled widely, backpacking her way round Europe, Africa, North and South America, and hitchhiking though Asia and New Zealand before falling in love with Australia. Its countryside, differing landscapes and animals enthralled Maricy and she decided to stay and felt so 'at home' she became a naturalised Australian citizen.

Working in security, the sports industry, traffic control and as a cleaner, Maricy eventually purchased a triangular block of land in Coraki, in northern New South Wales to house her horse. She set about building a shed and a dam on her three acres so that he has shelter and water, she visits regularly from the Gold Coast with her dog and best friend, Della, to ensure all is well.

Her life-long love of animals has led to Maricy volunteering at the Australian Bat Clinic and Currumbin Wildlife Hospital and be actively involved in the Animal Welfare League, her favourite organisation, as she has seen them all do such wonderful work with animals. It goes without saying that Maricy has been a vegetarian for a long time.

CONTENTS

Chapter 1   The Walk 1

Chapter 2   Choco-chip. 38

Chapter 3   Lucky 68

Chapter 4   Charlie the Brumby 82

Chapter 5   Jonesy. 96

Chapter 6   Matt's Small Engine Repairs 118

Chapter 7   New Start 130

Chapter 8   Morris the Cowboy 150

Chapter 9   Cozy Roland. 159

Chapter 10 Covering Ground. 175

Chapter 11 Homeward Bound 201

Glossary 221

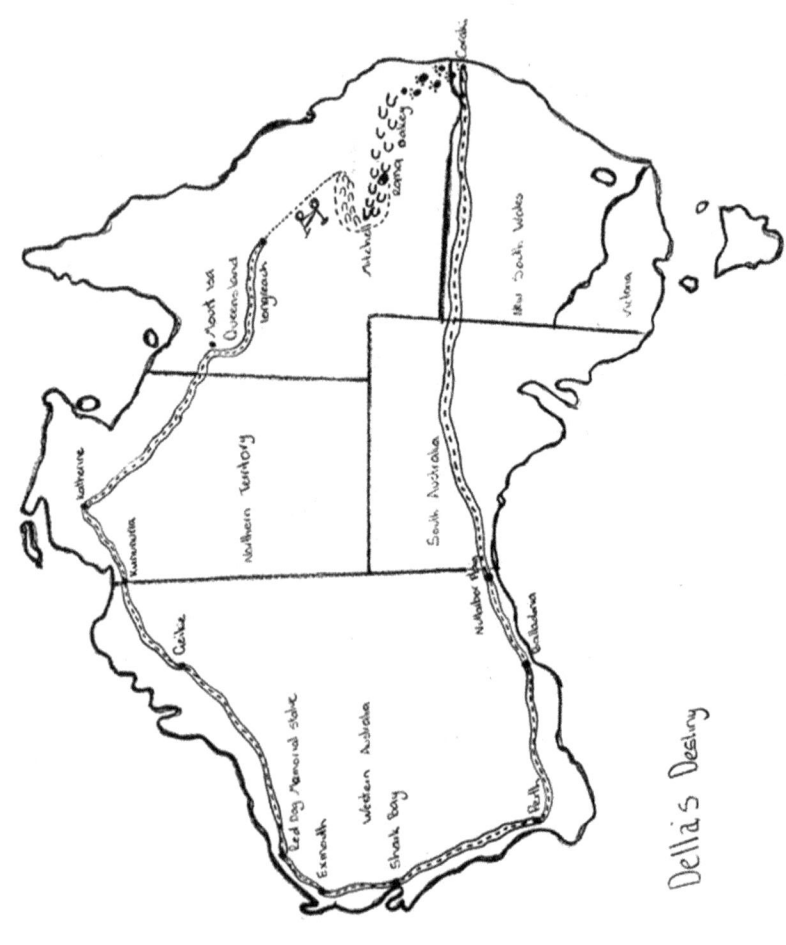

Della's Destiny

Introduction

I don't know if Della speaks English or I speak dog but we understand one another. We're very close, best mates in fact, and talk often. Della told me she loves me unconditionally, even on those days when I'm in a bad mood, but people don't always grasp this because I'm a tall dark-blonde woman and she's a black and white Border collie Cattle-dog. I adopted Della two years ago from the Animal Welfare League when she was just seven months old.

Our adventure started, when Della informed me she wanted to take a walk and go visit Red Dog. She loves the Red Dog movie and going for walks but we live in New South Wales and Red Dog lived in Dampier, Western Australia - a very long walk indeed. I quite liked the idea...why not, I thought? *It'd be an adventure.*

After considering the distance we would be trekking, I realised that, if we made the decision to go, we would need to bring Lucky, our four year-old gelding, along to help carry our supplies. Lucky is an adopted standard-bred harness racing horse, bay with a black mane and tail and has a gentle disposition.

I started by researching on the internet and reading books by others that had made similar trips. I sought out and talked to people who offered a heap of helpful and educational advice. I ended up contacting my two favourite charities - Animal Welfare League (AWL) and People for

The Ethical Treatment of Animals (PETA), and decided to change my 'mad walk across Oz' to a charity trip.

I should also mention, that I didn't partake in any physical training before starting off on this trip. So yes, anyone can do it. Along with the advice, I received heaps of negativity. Not 'Wow, what an exciting adventure you're going to have?' but 'Why?', 'You're crazy', 'You're going to die' and 'You're mad.' However, the remarks became more complimentary when I explained it was a charity walk, confirming that most people love animals. I produced a brochure setting out my walking route and requesting donations to the charities.

Before leaving on our walk across Australia, Lucky, Della and I thought it would be a good idea to get a taste of what lay ahead. We completed two trial runs; the first practice day was down Lagoon Road, with Lucky carrying half of our gear in his pack saddle and Della carrying her special doggie pack weighing about two kilos.

The second trial was an overnight run to Evans Head, New South Wales. We walked through Woodburn with most of the gear on Lucky whilst Della rehearsed carrying her pack. We camped by the beach at Evans Head and the next day walked back home.

Having had two successful walking trials, we started our walk of about 5,000 kilometres to Western Australia on September 3, 2012. I arranged for a mate, Yasmin Sayer, to mail prepacked, post-paid packages to me as and when I needed them and decided to keep a diary to document my walk.

On any walk such as this, one needs to prepare so I gathered advice on the weather and supplies I would need, reading library books written by people who had undertaken horse packing trips and talking to people who had expertise in walking Australia. I read up on snakes, spiders and plants poisonous to horses and humans – of which there are a hell of a lot in Australia - and determined I would stay away from all of them! 'The Colour of Courage' by Sharon Muir Watson gave me the basic information on how to undertake my trip the 'old fashioned way' using a horse to carry the supplies. I intended to follow the cattle stock routes – Mitchell, Longreach, Mount Isa, and Broome to Dampier, Western Australia.

Working and animals taking much of my time, I spent my little leisure hours sourcing the items. I soon found that many of the shops, that sold the equipment, employed sales people who never used their products, so I needed to thoroughly research everything before I shopped. I found I would need a special horse pack-saddle, swag, and dried food bags. A collapsible five-gallon water-bucket was high on my list of supplies and equipment. I couldn't lug around sufficient water for my horse Lucky, who can drink ten gallons of water in one go but I could carry sufficient water for a day's supply for me and my dog Della. I found I also used the bucket to wash clothes in, and in emergencies for Lucky (if the bank was too steep for him to get access to the water below). It's the best investment ever and only cost $7. Mountain Designs employed people who actually use their products and I purchased my thermals, waterproof spray, and sleeping bag from them. I bought a 'Driza Bone' oilskin jacket and a special whistle to call Della to heel. I purchased a 'Steripen' to make dirty water safe to drink and Berocca tablets for health. Slowly the supplies arrived from Outfitters Supply in Montana. I had studied the weather and figured when would be the best time of year to travel but, in hind-sight, should have started a month or so earlier because it ended up getting real hot in the outback! I took a mobile phone, donated by Ross Taverna of Telstra and a GPS that showed lakes, creeks, rivers and could estimate how far we would need to walk to water. Once further out west, I followed the drovers map and camped near the water points.

I had no real over-night stops planned and I didn't really worry about where I would camp.

Occasionally I met people who would arrange for me to camp on a mate's property or notify the local showground that I was coming and ask if I could stay there, as long as the places were in the direction of my journey.

I soon found that it took ninety minutes to pack both Lucky and Della. Lucky with the supplies that we needed for the trip (he was carrying eighty per cent of the goods) but it took only one minute to place Della in her harness and load her doggie pack on her back. Each morning I would have to pack my swag and everything I had brought with me and each night I would be unpacking my swag, settling Della and Lucky before turning in for the night. Chris Allen, a saddler at Horseland in Lismore fitted Lucky's pack saddle, which was bought from Outfitters Supply. It took three fittings to make sure the saddle fitted properly. To ensure my horse had room to feed and move around at night, at least thirty meters, I placed Lucky on a picket line (a rope with a hook each end) – (one end attached to a swivel metal U hook-ring on a stake), hammered into the ground, the other end attached to a hobble around the horse's ankle.

On the trip, I found Della didn't need a lead. She knew where to walk, just ahead on the grass, not on the road. I only had to take care of Lucky and let me tell you, I found it took a lot of care. I had to make sure the saddle didn't slip to one side and when it did, readjust it by tightening the pack saddle. I had to make sure Lucky didn't pick up a stone, causing him to limp in pain.

Many things happened to inspire me on my walk. One instance, was a lovely older widow trying to run a cattle station on her own. Although her house was very clean, it looked pretty bare inside and it was clear this lady, with old-fashioned manners like my Grandma, didn't have much and was 'doing it hard'. She was thin and frail but offered me a bed in her house and food from her bare cupboards…and I mean bare! Those cupboards were empty and I tried to insist I should cook my own food, but she wouldn't hear of it, stating it was only polite that I eat her meal, while apologising for not having any meat. Being a vegetarian, I told her not to worry. She picked vegetables from her garden and served up the freshly cooked vegetables. It was the loveliest dinner I had in my whole life, because I knew just how much it was worth to her. Even though people may have paid for my meal at a pub, this meal was worth more to me because she had nothing at all to give. On the way out the next morning, she tried to donate ten dollars but I refused and told her to use it to buy hay for her cattle. There was a drought and the grass wasn't growing. 'We can't be letting your animals suffer because other animals are' I told her, knowing she couldn't afford the money.

At Evans Head on one of our trial runs, a local called the newspaper and they sent out a photographer who stopped us on the side of the road to take pictures. I soon realised that local people who stopped to talk to me would contact the media to approach me, so that I didn't have to waste my time trying to gain the media's attention – a necessity for a charity walk. This happened throughout the weeks of my walk - we had our photos and articles about us in several local newspapers - until I had several misadventures and, despite my planning, ending up travelling faster than I had intended. The interest in my charity walk gradually dropped off despite my leaflets requesting a travelling companion – leaving the last number off my phone number probably didn't help!

This is my story.

Chapter One
The Walk

The morning we were to start, Monday 3rd September 2012, I began to hear all these negative voices in my head whilst loading Lucky. I noticed I had begun to shake nervously and it took a great deal of concentration to keep the apple I had for breakfast in my stomach. *Will this be the last time I see my home in Coraki? Will Lucky and Della be okay?* These worries swirled around in my head while I readied to leave. In the early morning light, I packed Lucky and Della. We left Coraki with Lucky and Della walking along the grass on the side of the road whilst I walked on the bitumen. Lagoon Road is a quiet and pleasant road. I soon became lost in its natural serenity, forgetting my worries about the walk ahead.

As I relaxed, I began to appreciate the flock of beautiful red and green brightly colourful lorikeets flying around, followed by a bunch of pink cockatoos. When Lucky spotted a kangaroo in a paddock it spooked him so much that he jumped before standing rooted to the spot. I talked soothingly to reassure him…*it's just a kangaroo.* On the other hand, Della was jumping around. She looked keen to give chase, but I told her, in no uncertain terms,

'No chasing the poor kangaroo, Della'. The sun shone through the trees and we were cooled by a delightful breeze as we continued on our way. The bitumen road became one lane of dirt and metal cattle grids. To avoid Lucky's hooves becoming caught in the grating, we walked around the cattle grids and through the gates located on the side of the road, we made sure to close the gates so the cattle couldn't escape. (Leaving gates as we found them is a very important rule that I learned from my research about pack-horse travel.)

Della and Lucky by the Richmond River

Some nine kilometres into our trek, a farmer riding a quad bike came into sight. I waved and he pulled over for a chat, introducing himself. His name was Petr and he ran a thousand acre station housing sheep and cattle. I told him of our plans and he explained the road we were on ended in another farm a kilometre further on. He told me

PETA was unpopular with sheep farmers and suggested not to mention them. PETA had stopped 'mulesing', a controversial practice of reducing 'flystrike' by removing strips of skin from sheep's' buttocks. Petr's invitation to his home for morning tea, and a talk about my options in walking to Casino, was gratefully accepted and he gave us all a nice respite.

On the front porch at his house, Petr sat and drew a map on how to get to Reynolds Road. It appeared we had about three kilometres of bush walking that included two double and one single gates. Thanking him for this new information and his hospitality, I headed out with Lucky & Della. In the first paddock, a beautiful white horse drew close to say hello. Lucky returned the greeting briefly and we continued walking. A few minutes later, Lucky dropped to the ground. My first thought was, *oh no I've overloaded him and he's collapsed.* I stopped and stared in horror, but soon realised that he was just trying to have a roll on the grass. Lucky soon figured out he couldn't roll with the pack on his back and got to his feet, but five minutes later he tried again. This time I didn't panic as I knew what he was trying to do. Once he realised the pack wasn't removed that easily, he gave up and stood upright. In the paddock, Della behaved well and stayed just ahead of us but Lucky pulled on the lead, insisting on smelling each and every pile of horse poo we came upon. *Yuk! What's so interesting about horse poo?*

At the end of the paddock, we came across an unexpected fourth gate. We walked through the gate and started down the dirt road. We stopped at a stream running next to the road where Della and Lucky paused to drink the clear water. Della wanted to go for a swim, but I held her back since she carried her backpack and didn't need to get it wet. Lucky seemed far more interested in eating the tall green grass growing beside the stream than drinking the water. We took a left turn when we reached the bitumen covered Coraki-Casino Road and walked along the side, making for Coopers Lane as Petr had mentioned it would be a good place to camp because of the nearby lake. Just when I thought I couldn't go any further, a white SUV pull in front of us. Out jumped a familiar face. It was Petr who said 'Wow, you got a lot farther than I thought you would, you walk fast. Just ahead is Coopers Lane.' Wishing us luck, he drove off. We turned into Coopers Lane and walked till cattle stockyards came into sight and I felt it would be a good place to camp. I opened the gate into the cattle-yard and began unloading Lucky as the noise of a cattle truck approached us. I waved it down and asked the driver permission to camp overnight. He informed me that the yards belonged to a guy named Steven. The driver gave him a call to see if camping would be okay, which it was. The driver advised me that our next overnight stop the following day should be at his mates place. 'After the bridge, look out for the second house on the left, the one that has a '**Whispering Pines**' sign out front.'

I checked Lucky's hooves for rocks and placed him on the picket line while the cows ambled over. Startled, Lucky began to bolt but he came to an abrupt halt when he got to the end of the picket line and almost toppled over. I ran up and talked calmly, while petting him and fed him some grain to take his mind off the cattle. Soon he had calmed down and I tried to chase the snooping cows away but they wouldn't budge – they just stood there looking at me. So I took out a carriage whip, given to me by saddler Chris, and cracked it on the ground, which made the cows take off. I didn't want the cows tucking into Lucky's grain or stepping on my swag in the middle of the night. Della was instructed on where to sleep - she has a special blue waterproof-backed flannel blanket - and I placed her food bowl on the corner of the blanket. After my meal, I settled into my swag. Around midnight, I woke and moved Lucky's picket line so he would have fresh grass to eat. Della was up and about doing her growling to keep the curious cows away. I told Della to get back on her blanket and try to get some sleep since we had another big walk tomorrow. I didn't want Della to overwork herself, walking and carrying her pack all day plus being a guard dog at night.

When I woke next morning, it was so cold. My feet were very sore and I put blister pads on them. Most of my toes were bleeding from the previous days' walking, so I swapped shoes. Packing the swag, bags and loading up Lucky took a while, but we were on the road at 8am, heading for Casino. In the absence of trees to cover the bitumen road, there was no shade and the day became increasingly hotter. It was a hard slog and those negative voices from the past began to raise their head. Ahead of us, a white car stopped on the opposite side of the road and a lady left the car and walked across and asked to take our photo. She stated she had seen me on the news and gave me a donation of $20. Our first donation! It lifted my spirits while we posed for a photo. Wow, I was so happy! I thanked her and we continued walking until we arrived at road works. The traffic controller said he had never stopped a horse before, but that there is a first time for everything! All the road-workers stopped as we walked past them on the side of the road. Maybe the workers were surprised and too busy staring to work or perhaps they were being kind, not wanting their loud equipment to startle Lucky.

A few kilometres later, Farmer Petr's SUV pulled up and he handed me an orange juice, apple, mandarin, and banana saying 'Happy Birthday.' I thanked him for remembering (when talking at his farm, I had mentioned the following day was my birthday). Delighted, I ushered us under a nearby tree in front of an abandoned house for a short break. Lucky ate the long grass on the side of the road and Della looked longingly at the cows in the paddock, wanting to chase them. I checked the outside tap on the side of the house and it worked, so filled the water bucket for Lucky and Della. Della drank thirstily but Lucky wasn't too interested. After a rest, we continued on our walk but we hadn't gone far when I noticed that Lucky had begun to limp. I stopped to check his hooves and found a rock, embedded in manure, in his front right hoof, the one he had been favouring. I removed it with my horse-pick, and observed him carefully, happy to see he now walked fine. We arrived at a small bridge, but Lucky just wouldn't cross. He stopped and braced himself, telling me 'No way'. I was puzzled, as we'd never had a problem before with other bridges we had crossed on our travels. Then I remembered the carrots I had saved in his nosebag that was tied around my waist. I pulled out a carrot and held it in front of him and started walking very fast. Lucky seemed to forget his fear of the bridge and chased me to try to get that carrot. I allowed him a few bites on the way over the bridge as an encouragement and he truly deserved that carrot after all the walking he had done. I calculated that we must be approaching **Whispering Pines** and looked for the sign. We were tired, I had blisters and Lucky was ready to call it a day. I spotted the sign in front of a small brick house. I tied Lucky to the white fence just outside the cattle grid and Della and I walked up the driveway to the front door and knocked. An older lady opened the door. Her expression told me she seemed real suspicious. I explained the cattle driver had suggested we might be able to camp in her yard. Her husband joined us and I repeated the cattle driver's suggestion, explaining my trip. The couple introduced themselves as Jack and Peggy Ferguson. Jack agreed I could camp out in the back with Della and that Lucky could stay in the stockyards down the road. He walked down the driveway with us and I unloaded Lucky and dumped the gear at the end of his drive. Jack then drove down to the stockyards and met Lucky and I there. We filled the water trough and left the horse in the grassy yard with Lucky's grain-filled nosebag on the ground. Della and I hopped in Jack's SUV and loaded the gear in the back of the vehicle.

Jack Ferguson and Lucky

Jack Ferguson was really keen to look at my gear and watch me set up the swag. He and Peggy offered the use of their shower. Oh, bliss, a hot shower and Peggy washed my clothes too! With clean clothes and a clean body I began to feel better already, despite my blisters! The couple invited me in for a chat and insisted that I eat dinner with them. Having a hot meal prepared for me was terrific and when they found it was my birthday, they insisted I stay for another day so Peggy could make me her special Mississippi Mud Cake. Peggy always looked for an excuse to have chocolate, so I agreed to stay another day. That night, I watched a video with them in their lounge but couldn't keep my eyes open for long. Yawning, I returned to the back yard and Della. She was there, tail wagging, waiting for me on her blanket and I crawled into my swag, replete, refreshed, and happily went to sleep. I slept well but it was a cold night and I didn't get out of my swag till 7am. I started organising my stuff and Jack came out of the house to tell me that breakfast was ready. I replied that I don't eat breakfast, but Peggy had made toast and baked beans for me, so he explained I had better go in and eat. After eating breakfast, the Fergusons suggested our next stay overnight should be in the yard of their mate in O'Conners Lane. I wanted to see if Lucky needed anything so Jack, Della and I walked to the stockyards to visit him. Lucky seemed quite content enjoying the long grass. Jack showed us around his property and we checked out the chooks, which took Della's interest but I told her no chasing was allowed. A reporter, Janelle McLennan, arrived from the local Casino newspaper to interview me about my charity walk. We sat on the front porch and talked until Janelle drove Della and I down to the stockyards to take photos with Lucky. Lucky closely followed me around the yard and Janelle took a few photos for her article. After she left, I joined the Fergusons in the lounge, ate a piece of the delicious mud cake that Peggy made for me (she even sang me 'happy birthday'), and finished watching the Scottish video from the night before. Later, after dinner, Peggy called Ruthie from O'Conner's Lane to see if I could camp in her yard. I think it was due to Jack talking her ear off about me but Ruthie agreed.

It was 5:50am and windy when I awoke the next morning. I felt nervous because we had a long 24-kilometre walk ahead of us. There was no dew on the ground and it seemed quite mild. Lucky, Della and I walked back to the end of Jack's driveway. Jack had driven his SUV over the cattle grid with my gear, so I wouldn't have to carry it. With Jack's help it didn't take long to load Lucky and my present, a handy folding-stool Jack had given me. I hugged the wonderful Fergusons goodbye and we started off down the road. We got to Casino really quickly, walking alongside the beautiful Richmond River. We went past a school and a small girl stopped us. She asked to pat Lucky, but I told her she should pat Della because Lucky was nervous of people he didn't know. (He had jumped when some school kids from Coraki patted him. Della is more agreeable to pats). We continued on to the Casino Hospital lawn and stopped so I could take off my oilskin. Wearing it had made me feel quite hot and I took the opportunity to readjust Lucky's packsaddle. I worry about his comfort and it is sometimes hard to get the balance right. We took a few breaks along Summerland Way, including a picture with the Casino sign. I was sitting on Jack's stool having a break when a man pulled up and left his car to walk over and scrutinize Lucky's gear. We chatted and when I explained I had stayed at the

Fergusons' he said that he knew Jack. He confided that he used to be a jockey and was really keen on horses gear and that had caused him to stop. On this road there was an upsetting amount of road-kill. So many animals had been hit and we passed a dead lizard, possum, owl, turtle, and a kangaroo. In the heat of the sun, they really started to smell and I could tell we were going to come across something dead, long before it came in sight. There was so much trash along the road too - strange things like a seatbelt buckle, a purple vibrator, playing cards, scissors, and lots of CDs and DVDs. Lucky was startled the first time he stepped on a soda can but soon became used to it and strode through the trash like one does at the end of a Big Day Out. Eventually I found a shady spot in front of a cattle-yard gate and took a long break. Della managed to take her pack off all by herself and proceeded to run around sniffing everything. Continuing our walk, about two kilometres along, I spotted a man out the front of his house and asked if we could have some water. At the same time, a grey SUV pulled up and a man got out and opened the back, bringing out a green 20 litre plastic water jerry can for Lucky and Della. Then he brought out cups for us and some sort of lemon drink to keep up my energy. How thoughtful was that? He said his mother walked the BNT trail for a while and he knew it was hard going.

We continued our walk and made it to Ruthie's place around early afternoon and she immediately offered me her spare room to sleep in. I settled Lucky in the paddock with some grain, fed Della, then went inside and had a shower…heaven! Ruthie's cooking was great and dinner was delicious; I even had second helpings with passionfruit and ice cream for dessert. Full of food, clean and exhausted, I slept like a log. I climbed out of that blissful bed at 6am the next morning and loaded up. We were on the road by 7:50am after I hugged Ruthie goodbye. She had been so compassionate and I thanked her for her hospitality. The day started out cool, windy, and pleasant but began to heat up very quickly and I soon took off my oilskin jacket. We had quite a few breaks along the way and saw a long snake that had been hit by a vehicle, on the side of the road. It was a very big snake - when stretched out it would have covered both lanes easily. We stopped at Cedar Point Hall for water and Della and I sat at the picnic table while Lucky ate grass. Shortly after leaving there, Ruthie pulled up in her ute with water for Lucky and Della. I explained that they had just been watered and we'd had a good break and were doing fine. I was overwhelmed to think she had driven to help us and thanked her warmly for her concern and efforts.

When we arrived at Kyogle, we had an uphill climb so I stopped at the first park we passed and gave Della and Lucky a water break. Della was keen on the water but Lucky seem more interested in the clover. I guessed the hill took more out of me than them! Resuming our walk through the west side of town to the Kyogle Showground, we made our way to Denis the caretakers' house where he said he was expecting us. He showed us the paddock Lucky could stay in and pointed out the land beside it where we could camp and I paid the $10 overnight fee. While I relaxed in the shade after unpacking Lucky and Della, Darryl showed up. Darryl explained he travels round Australia, working as a relief station caretaker, living in his 5th wheel mobile home. He was staying at the Showground, and gave me advice on where to camp. I showered and washed my clothes in the shower, hanging them to dry on the fence where they dried quickly because of the sun and wind. Feeling hungry, but not wanting to eat by myself, I took my dried food bag to Darryl, who'd been so friendly, and ate my dinner with him - he had cold cuts and I had my Nasi Goreng. My meal was surprisingly good and I ate the whole meal, which I hadn't done before. Darryl offered ice cream & fruit for dessert, but I declined and headed off to my swag. I blew Della's whistle as she was running around the campground and I wanted her next to me while I slept. I woke up early because of the cold and quickly loaded Lucky and Della. It seemed easier today as I felt well and the bags were lighter in weight. As we headed out of the Showground, we had our photo taken by Darryl and a neighbour camper who wished us luck. We headed north on Summerland Way at 7:50am. Our early morning break was taken along the side of the highway; in the long grass so Lucky could eat his fill and I could have a drink and a protein bar. I started to eat an apple but Lucky came along and snatched it away, eating it before it could be retrieved. We returned to the road and a blonde, bare-footed lady jumped out of her car (she said she was a farrier) to take a look at Lucky's hooves. She was happy to tell me they were in good condition and during our chat, suggested we stay at the Wiangararee Showground instead of the rest area that Darryl recommended, saying she would leave a biscuit of hay at the cattle-yard gate for Lucky. Thanking her profusely we continued on our way.

Half an hour later a car pulled up carrying familiar faces. Alison and Russell (who are Gold Coast friends) brought carrots that Russell fed to Lucky. I received cookies, various fruits including strawberries and fruity filled nut bars. Lucky always has a sniff to see what's available and usually manages to steal the fruit. When we arrived at the Showground, I went directly to the stockyards and unsaddled Lucky and Della, and found the hay the lady Farrier had left for Lucky. Not finding any water, I walked Lucky and Della across the highway to the lake. Della immediately jumped in and swam around while Lucky had a good long drink. I needed to refill my water bottles and didn't want to use the lake water so we walked over to the next-door farm and one of the men turned the water pump on for me. We had a bit of a chat about my trip and they suggested, the following night, we stay with Fred who owned the old mill in Grevillia. I thanked them for the information and filled my water bottles and Lucky's trough. After showing Della the water's location, I returned to our supplies and ate some of my friend Alison's delicious homemade cookies and plump strawberries. The next morning, I started my usual routine of folding the swag and packing Lucky and we were on the road by 7:30am. After an hour into the walk, Lucky decided that he didn't want to go on anymore. So the first thing I did was to check his hooves and made sure there were no stones causing him pain. Next, I had to make sure the pack saddle was fitted properly and didn't rub anywhere. Everything seemed fine, but Lucky didn't want any part of this adventure anymore. The grain bribe worked for a while, but an hour later he pulled away from me and trotted to the fence to eat grass. It was just so frustrating, I tried the grain, carrots and then holding his halter but he just put his head up and yanked away from me. So, since all else had failed, I reluctantly had to get out the whip Chris had given me. I hit the side of the packsaddle and Lucky walked on. The road was pleasant and the scenery lovely, but I couldn't enjoy it properly since I was too busy focusing on getting Lucky moving.

Every step was an effort, my arms hurt and my feet ached. He kept dragging me down to the grassy area by the fence. I couldn't walk in the long grass with all the uneven ground but he continued pulling up and stopping.

We finally arrived at Old Grevillia where there was a house with many children out front and camper vans. A man came out of one and said that I could give some of his water to my horse and dog. We walked into the yard and both Della and Lucky drank out of the trough. Some of the children had mullet haircuts and all the children were barefoot and I thought they looked like very 'hillbilly' type of people. I thanked them and we went on our way to New Grevillia. Our arrival at Fred and Colleen's house was much later than I anticipated, due to Lucky's bad behaviour. They showed us where to camp and invited us in. They were a very friendly couple and they were having a Sunday session with their mates. I unloaded Lucky and gave him some grain and their miniature horses came over and started helping themselves to my supplies. I thought the little fellows were very badly behaved but they were so cute – being just a little bigger than Della - I couldn't get mad at them. Lucky was forced to share his grain and they stole Alison's apple from my plastic bag. I had to grab my bag and tried to shoo them away but the tiny horses were way too curious and wanted to sniff everything. Fred came over with a stick and chased the miniature horses away so that I was free to attach the nose-bag of grain to Lucky's head. Poor Lucky was chased around by the miniature horses trying to gain access to his out-of-reach nose bag. Fred gave me a tour of his art gallery, bike museum, coffee shop, workshop, and house. I could see a lot of thought went into Fred's self-built constructions. I removed Lucky's nose bag and shut him in a paddock with the llamas who weren't bugging Lucky like the little horses. In the morning, it was so cold my fingers froze while I buckled Lucky's packsaddle. Gradually the temperature warmed up and weather-wise, it became a great day, not too hot and just right for walking. Lucky began acting up around 9:30am so we had a break, with Lucky eating the grass and me an apple and one of Alison's nut bar. We took off again and the same thing happened - Lucky just didn't want to go. I pulled, I tried bribery but nothing worked for long and I became very frustrated! We dragged on and met a guy who said Glen Road was just 5 kilometres away. So we took a water and food break at the empty fruit stand at the end of Hildrebrand Road, using the last of our water since we were almost at the lake and would be able to get more there. We never made it. Lucky just wouldn't go anymore. He kept pulling away and running into the Unumgar State Forest with me having to go down the embankment to catch him. Then I had to pull him back up onto the road. By mid-afternoon, after the fifth time, I was exhausted and I just couldn't fight him any longer. I tied him to a tree in the forest and set up camp, with no water. I sprayed all of us with Bushman's insect repellant, gave Della some wet and dry dog food, I had a nut bar, and Lucky had a nose bag of grain for dinner. I managed to find a little water in one of the bottles and gave it to Della and we went to sleep in the bug filled forest and I turned off my alarm. I didn't want to wake up early to this problem of getting Lucky out of the forest!

I woke at six and broke camp, luring Lucky out of the forest with the last of the grain. He followed but when he got to the road he didn't want to walk. It occurred to me that the gravel might be hurting his hooves. After much effort, using the grain bribes, pulling on the lead rope, and using the whip, I finally got Lucky moving along, and once I got him walking I soon realised we had been less than a kilometre from where we were supposed to camp! We toddled into the cow paddock with the lake and I unloaded Lucky and we all had a long cold drink. Della jumped right in and then rolled around in the mud. I was busy putting Lucky in hobbles so he could graze and I looked up to see a strange brown grey dog staring back. Startled, I returned the stare, wondering why Della wasn't chasing the strange dog away from me, when I noticed a pink name-tag on its neck and realised it was, in fact, Della. I've never seen Della a different colour before but all I was worried about was her coming over to me for a pat! She read my mind, and jumped on me for a cuddle. I pushed her away but the damage was done, my black jeans were now brown! I then began the process of filtering the muddy cow lake water, using my Steripen to make it drinkable. It still tasted like I was drinking dirty watered-down mud. So I added a Berocca tablet to it to make it more palatable. After a couple of hours rest, I loaded Lucky and we went on our way. It was a shady dirt-road and Lucky and Della walked on the grass whilst I walked on the road. Lucky seemed a bit better today, and I began to hope that we might reach the Woodenbong Showground that night. Della was definitely walking along smelling the roses, as the saying goes. When I wasn't busy pulling Lucky, I would glance at Della and she would be just walking, sniffing her way along the walk, stopping at trees, bushes, clumps of grass, and of course she had to smell all the poo (there was a lot of cow manure on the side of that road).

Bimbi Creek Rd. was very shady and hilly, but the grass along the side was perfect for Lucky's tired hooves. He behaved and walked fine along that road until we came upon a lady watering her plants with the garden hose in front of her house on Glennie St. We chatted as I stopped and filled Lucky's bucket with water. I emptied out my muddy water from my bottles and refilled it with the fresh clear water. This happy scene turned to disaster as Lucky's head suddenly jerked up from his water bucket. His head hit the lady in the face. I felt awful for her. Lucky didn't care he'd hurt her face and started to eat her manicured lawn. I apologised profusely and left quickly. We passed a petrol station and a lady came out to meet us stating she was expecting us. She pointed us in the right direction and explained that a Darren & Megan had brought food for Lucky. Since Lucky had eaten the rest of his grain that morning it was a relief to know he had food waiting. When we arrived at the Showground, Lucky went in hobbles after being unloaded and I set up camp. I filled up my solar camp shower for the first time and stood gratefully under a tepid shower. I still had drinking water, which was lucky, as the water had been turned off at the Showgrounds. I un-hobbled Lucky and put him in the paddock to eat the grass. The next morning I didn't get out of my swag early. I knew we were waiting there for Lucky's 'Simple Boots' to be delivered. I hand-washed my clothes with soap in Lucky's foldable drinking bucket and hung the wet clothes over the railing to dry. A couple pulled up in their car and I became excited as I thought it was Darren & Megan. It was a different couple, Rod & Liz, who had arrived to feed and ride their horses in the paddock on the other side of the stream. They gave me advice on which road to take to Killarney and turned the Showground water on for me, filling up the water trough. Lucky was put back in the paddock while the couple rode their horses around. He watched and became excited when they were being ridden. I wondered if this was a sign Lucky might be happy to carry me instead of the supplies. With the water turned on, I took the opportunity to have a proper shower with my camp shower. Now clean and refreshed, Della was tied up to protect the gear while I walked to the petrol station and had lunch. I felt guilty for leaving her so I only ate half and brought the rest back for her with a can of dog food and another bag of dry dog food. She didn't act like she missed me all that much when I returned. She'd been having a snooze in the shade instead of being a guard dog but when she woke she was terribly interested in what I had in the plastic bag and had no problem finishing my lunch. Not long after, Darren and Megan showed up with Lucky's food: carrots, apples, pony pellets, and hay and he tore into it right away. I cut up the apples for him but he obviously didn't feel like them and went back to eating the grass in the paddock. The couple confided that they take in neglected farm animals. They have fifty animals that need homes – geese, horses, donkeys, roosters, goats, sheep and many more. Della liked the couple a lot and tried licking their faces. Around 9pm, my mate Paul arrived with Lucky's 'Simple Boots' and a bag of grain. I started stressing right away because I realised I had incorrectly taken his hoof measurements. With trepidation, I measured Lucky's hoof and tried a boot on him…and it fitted. The gel pads made for the inside of the boots were a bonus. When I said goodbye, Paul talked me into keeping his very warm blanket and as I climbed into the swag, I realised he had also left two very huge pillows. I slept so well with the new pillows and blanket that I didn't have to put on my oilskin jacket in the middle of the night. However, while packing up in the morning, I barely managed to fit the blanket in one of the bags. I strapped the two pillows to the top of Lucky's pack but felt a little embarrassed to be seen leading Lucky around carrying fluffy pillows. *What would people think?* I tried my best to hide them under the bags, but it didn't really work. Lucky wore his boots and loved them. He seemed to want to walk on the bitumen to hear his hooves go clip clop but I insisted he walk on the grass. This went well, no misbehaving at all – he plowed along like a trooper. It had taken me so long to figure it out but I was relieved and wished I could read his mind. He could have told me he needed boots a few days ago and I would have bought them sooner. He did eighteen kilometres 'breaking in' his new boots on the first day. We took the locals' advice and walked down the Mount Lindsay Highway with a beautiful uphill windy walk through the shady Bald Knob State Forest. The weather was perfect and the Highway very quiet and everyone slowed down when they spotted us on the road. I filled Lucky's water bucket from a cow trough but had to climb through a barbed-wire fence to get to it and snagged my jeans, leaving a hole. We only had two short breaks along the way as I wanted to keep the momentum going since Lucky had walked along so well, and I didn't want to jinx it. I began looking for water again around 2pm and we walked along a creek that led to a 'Hotham Park' sign. So we pulled up and I filled the water bucket from the stream. As usual, Della jumped into the creek and went for a swim. I decided to camp there for the night. Lucky had 'done good' in his new boots and I didn't want him to overdo it. The park had plenty of clover and grass cover so I put Lucky in his hobbles – he could get around and eat what he wanted. While setting up camp, a 1929 year red convertible pulled up and a man got out and ate his lunch. So I had a chat with the man who introduced himself as Alan Geldard. Alan told me the most amazing story about his car. He'd bought a green car and mentioned it to his dad who replied that he'd owned a red car in the same model before Alan was born. Whilst fixing it up and painting it, Alan had sanded it back and found red paint underneath. So Alan checked out the car's provenance. He worked backwards from whom he'd bought the car and his dad worked from who he sold the car to, and after many owners they both realised that this was the very same car his dad had owned! As I busied myself, a horse-float pulled up. Lindsay introduced himself explaining he managed cattle ranches in the area, so he was always back and forth. He lived in Woodenbong, so I asked him if he could stop by the Showground and collect the spare lead-rope I had accidentally left behind. I told him that I would be on this same road for two more days and that I'd had no mobile reception when I'd tried to text Rod & Liz. I'd climbed down to the creek three times to fill Lucky's water bucket – he just kept drinking and drinking. Della went along and had me throw her a stick in the creek – she just loves water – so she could swim after it. It started getting cold and so she would have her own little warm swag, I made a little bed for Della with pack-bags in a semi-circle, Lucky's horse pad on top and Della's blanket on the ground. During the night, it rained and hailed for about an hour. It kept me awake but I felt relieved and glad Della would be dry in her little area. After the storm, I scrambled to check on everyone and found both Della and Lucky asleep. Lucky was laying down, which came as a surprise since I'd never known Lucky to lay down to sleep.

Next morning, I climbed out of the swag, and it felt freezing. In the shade of the trees the temperature had dropped. I decided to leave the pillows in the swag and fold it up with the pillows inside. Now people are going to think that my swag is big enough to fit all three of us in it. My fingers froze while trying to pack Lucky. My fingers were so cold I couldn't feel them moving and had to look at them to see if they were working correctly. To warm them up, I put my hands inside Lucky's upper rear leg for a minute so I could finish packing. As I packed, Lindsay stopped by and brought my lead rope and I thanked him profusely. I put a full nose bag on Lucky and hobbled him. He still moved around a bit, but I didn't have anywhere to tie him up to. When we set off on the road, it had warmed slightly. I left my oilskin jacket on for most of the cool sunny day. A great deal of water remained in puddles along the road from the rain the previous night and Lucky and Della drank from that when they were thirsty. I climbed down an embankment to get a bucket of water for Lucky but despite my efforts, he didn't drink it. It had been a beautiful clear running creek so I kept the water and poured it into my water bottles. Della, of course followed me down to the creek and jumped in for a swim. I have to remember to always take Della's pack off before I go to a creek or lake, because I know she will jump in for a swim. Fred from Grevillia drove by in his ute and took a picture of us. It was good to see him again. After a steady uphill climb, we were halfway to the top, when Lucky decided to lay down and do a roll. When he got back up, the pack saddle had slipped to one side and then under his belly. As I tried to decide how to get the saddle off, a nice guy stopped his car and helped me unload Lucky and then reload him again. We travelled for three more kilometres and found a lake to camp by, but the gate was rusted shut. As we couldn't gain entry, we continued on the road and another gate, on the opposite side of the road, came in sight. I walked over to investigate and found I could open it and saw there was another lake in the paddock. Della was overjoyed to go for another swim. While I unloaded, I noticed that Chris' whip had fallen out. Lucky has been behaving, now that he has his boots and I haven't needed the whip. Lucky received a large nose bag of grain as a reward as he'd worked so hard climbing that huge mountain. Lucky woke me out of my swag the next morning by pawing at the ground with his hoof. I jumped out to see why and took him to the trough for water. He didn't want to drink so I guessed he wanted his morning grain, which he doesn't usually get till I'm ready to load him (he stands still eating while I pack him). I put him back on the picket line and began folding up the swag, this time I folded it with only one pillow in it, the one I'm going to keep. I put the second pillow on top, planning on mailing it back to Paul when I came across the next post office. Loading up took less time than usual, and we were on the road by 7:30am. The first two kilometres were all uphill then flattened out and went downhill. Rod and Liz stopped by the side of the road and we had a chat and they checked out Lucky's new boots. Continuing on our way, we came to the Post Office. I unloaded the extra pillow and rushed into the shop to the post counter and said 'I want to mail this.' The assistant replied 'not today'. I was shocked and asked 'why not?' She said 'it's Saturday'. My idea over-turned, I left the Post Office and we headed along the way to Killarney. Little traffic passed us and Lucky behaved very well and on this quiet road we passed the Queensland border sign. I took a photo; it was so good to have finally reached the border crossing and accomplish part of the walking plan. Finally it felt like we were making headway, although I knew we still had a long way to go.

Della and Lucky by the Queensland border

We pulled up into the grounds of Historical Society Building. I entered the building and asked if the Showground was open. The lady assistant phoned around to the Society's members, but she received no reply. I told her that I had to unload Lucky - I couldn't leave him standing there all day. I checked around and found a second entrance open and unloaded Lucky and put him in a grassy paddock. He rolled around on his back and then followed me around while I checked to make sure all the gates were closed. The lady from the historical society had called John from the local newspaper. He pulled up and I mentioned that I really needed a shower and to wash my clothes, so John suggested we visit a nearby caravan park. I tied Della to watch our supplies and John drove me to the caravan park we had passed. He said he would come the next morning to take our picture for the newspaper. Faye and Trevor who ran the park and were really friendly and they even offered Della and I a caravan to sleep in. A real bed – wow! I washed my clothes and hung them up and had a long hot shower. Feeling really good now, together we went over my maps and they helped me plan out the next few days of our trip. I loaded Lucky up in record time the next morning. No folding up a wet swag, no bush toilet, no getting water from the creek, no trying to get dressed without getting my clothes wet from the dew. Yahoo! I was on the road by 6.40am, the earliest time yet. John caught up in his car and said he would drive further down the road and take our photo as we walked towards him. We strolled through town on that quiet Sunday morning. John had us posing by the Killarney welcome sign, taking photos for his newspaper article. We waved goodbye and continued along until about 9am when a nice lady came out of her house and offered me a cuppa, so I accepted gratefully. Della slipped out of her pack and Lucky ate the grass whilst I had a Milo and chatted. Mary, a bank teller, was often on her own as her husband worked away in the mines although she seemed to want company we had to say farewell. The road was pretty level with only a few small hills and it felt really enjoyable walking it. There were swarms of pink cockatoos flying around and eating in fields. We came upon an abandoned house and went round the back to fill up the water bucket from the rainwater tank. On the road a little later, a friendly woman and her daughter stopped and offered to bring food from the nearby McDonalds. I ordered a chocolate milkshake and sure enough they returned a while later with my milkshake. We pulled into the Murray Bridge Primary School and I introduced myself to Cheryl, the principal, who was there with her husband. Cheryl, the only full time teacher for the school's fourteen students was readying the place for its seventy-fifth year anniversary. She made us feel welcome with a cup of tea, a cheese toasted sandwich and ginger cookies. Lucky ambled around the fenced in schoolyard looking for grass - without success as it had been cut short. I found him eating weeds and plants so I gave him grain. I had swapped the grain bag with my food bag, because Lucky had previously rubbed the waterproof pack against a barbed wire fence and poked a hole in his grain bag. I repaired it with electrical tape over the tear but was afraid it wouldn't hold for long since rain had been forecast the next day. The swag was set up in the lunch area under shelter in an effort to keep it away from the wet morning dew. Thankfully, in the morning everything was dry and I used the bathroom - a real toilet and a sink to brush my teeth and wash my hands. I was loaded up and on the road by 7am. The road ahead was pretty level and I could feel a chill in the air. Cheryl and one of her students stopped us on the road to wish me luck and I apologised for Lucky leaving a poo on her driveway, but she laughed and replied she would hose it off. Along the way, Lucky ate a lot of grass that day. On reflection, I was relieved he hadn't eaten the school shrubs and flowers as he'd had little grass to eat at the school. After our stop to buy grain, we turned a corner and Lucky's pack-netting caught on a stake and he panicked. I only had one glove on when he pulled away from me and my ungloved hand was caught. The rope twisted around my ungloved hand and gave me rope-burn. I thought my index finger was broken. Lucky ran onto the street and stopped abruptly. I collected him and walked him to a gate and tied him up to inspect the pack. He had snapped the elastic cord in the netting and he had another hole in his new grain sack. So now I had holes in two of the four waterproof bags. I patched the latest hole with electrical tape and crossed my aching fingers that it would work. We headed off again and it began to get very hot. My finger throbbed, so I took a break at a park. I gave the animals water and accessed the damage to my finger, which wasn't broken, just bruised. I checked the GPS and figured if we cut through Warwick instead of walking around it we would save some kilometres, so we headed down the New England Highway. This time we all walked on the grass as the ground was hard and level. We came across a caravan park and I asked if we could stay. The woman there agreed Lucky and I could camp but refused Della so we moved on.

It started to rain as the Condamine River Park came into sight. I put on my oilskin and I made camp. I set up the tarpaulin first, so Della had shelter as I know she hates rain. I placed Lucky on the picket line, and set up my swag before climbing in and waiting for the rain to pass. Both Della and I nodded off but the sun came out and its warmth woke us. I walked to the river, leaned over the embankment to fill the water bucket and lost my balance. The water didn't feel very cold but my shoes, socks and pants were soaking wet. Still, I was grateful I hadn't fallen in headfirst. I figured, since I was there, I might as well fill up the water bucket. I managed to cling to grass and tree-roots and pull myself out. Grateful that I had packed two pairs of shoes and pants, all I could think was *the stuff I go through to keep the animals watered!* I patted Lucky and checked him for ticks and only found one.

Next morning while in the swag, I heard Lucky's hobbles clinking too fast to be on a picket line. I found Lucky had taken this opportunity, with no one around, to break his picket line and wander into Rosehill Street. I grabbed the lead rope and ran after him, dragging him back to my swag. I put the hobbles back on him but didn't have anywhere to tie him up. He kept wandering towards the road and I had to keep going after him to bring him back. I was busy 'breaking up' camp but with Lucky being mischievous, I wasn't making headway. I tied his lead rope to Della's collar and told Della to keep him nearby. Poor Della was dragged off to wherever Lucky decided the grass looked tastier. This time I refilled the water bucket without falling into the river – a good thing as I was wearing the only pair of dry pants and boots left. Della walked in front of us on the grass (she has learned exactly where to walk). But stopped occasionally to put her nose against my leg, like she is saying 'hello' or just making sure it's still me. I'd say 'that's a good girl' and she'd wag her tail and get back into her 'correct' walking position. We passed a paddock that had a trough close to the road and an unlocked gate which I opened and led Della and Lucky into the paddock for a drink. (When we left and I shut the gate as any good walker should.) Our next stop was the Town Hall to refill my water bottles and give Lucky and Della a drink. Lucky tried to eat the wood on the ramp leading up to the entrance. A beautiful blonde lady stopped by in her four-wheel drive and had a chat, inviting me to stay at her place. A real bed in a real house sounded great and I really needed a shower. Above us a big storm was brewing so I quickly agreed and Heidi gave me directions to her house. We started down the Allora-Warwick Road with Heidi's house as our destination. This walk was terribly upsetting as the road had so much road-kill. Every kilometre we would pass a dead native animal, mostly kangaroos, and the stench was terrible. Unexpectedly Lucky began to be a bit more interested in our trip, insisting on stopping and smelling things - like a black rubber tire, a dead echidna, and even a soda can. I think Lucky's nose (his sense of smell anyway) didn't work well but stopping to smell the road kill, especially when I could smell it from afar, was a little too much. Even Della took a wide walk around the dead animals and didn't sniff them, while I held my breath till we passed. We finally made it to Heidi's house and found out it was just after 1pm which meant we had walked 23 kilometres that day. I felt pleased we were improving in our time and distance. I led Lucky into a round pen and Heidi gave him some biscuits of hay. She explained about showing Welsh & Cob horses and that she had arranged for her neighbours to come over for a 'barbie' to meet me. Heidi's friend, Lorelle came to visit after work and invited me to stop by her place for a break the next afternoon on my way to Clifton. Heidi started arranging for me to stay at the properties of members of her Welsh horse club. By the end of the night, I had the rest of my week planned out. I went to bed feeling extremely relieved that we had destinations where we would be welcomed and have water. Pre-dawn, where the sky just becomes grey, is the loveliest time in the morning. Because it had rained last night, I found Lucky's hooves were caked in thick black mud. I had to scrape away all that mud and ended up getting pretty dirty. I finally placed his boots on clean hooves. Then began the loading procedure and he began moving all over again. I tied him up short to the horse float, so he couldn't move about while I loaded him up. Heidi made Lucky some special mash but he didn't eat much of it. Maybe he was just too full - anyway I don't think he was too impressed with his breakfast. We were soon on the New England Highway heading north. It was a busy road but most of the way we kept to the tractor track alongside the road. Della and Lucky plowed through the deep grass and ruts with no problems. We did have to walk the highway for about two kilometres which meant a great deal of bush walking - very hard on my ankles and feet. I ended up leaning on Lucky's neck for about a kilometre. I dropped my arm over Lucky's neck and he supported some of my weight while he led the way. He helped me along, behaving well while he didn't try to stop to eat the grass. I think he could tell I was having problems walking in that terrain. We finally arrived at Spring Creek Road and stopped off at Lorelle's house. Heidi was there and unloaded Della while Lorelle and I unloaded Lucky and put in him a paddock. Inside the house for damper and a 'cuppa', I found Heidi had been round Allora that morning with my brochure collecting donations for AWL. I couldn't believe that someone would do something that wonderful. We left Lorelle's house and we walked on to Clifton and arrived at the Showground. Bruce, the caretaker, was so very welcoming and gave us the stockyards and the sale stables to stay in and even dropped off hay for Lucky. I felt quite fatigued and couldn't be bothered with setting up my swag for the night. I just slept in my sleeping bag on Lucky's pack pad but in the morning, it was so cold I didn't get out of the bag till 6am. Bruce came to say farewell while I was loading Lucky and gave me directions while opening the back gate for me. We had seen some horses training on the race track and Lucky became quite animated. It seemed a good time to run, so we ran for a while, while Lucky did his special trot (I think he just wanted to show off). Everything on his back jumped up and down and made noise. When we arrived at Nobby we found two girls with their father out front of a house and I asked for a bucket of water for Lucky and Della. The girls were delighted to pat Lucky while the animals drank thirstily. We said goodbye and toddled off across the street where there were a few trees. I sat down for a break and a lady came and took our picture. She invited us to the caravans, a bit farther down, so we went. All the motor-home people came out to have a chat and fed Lucky carrots, Della liver treats, and I received strawberries and a banana. I thanked them and we continued along our way down Nobby Connection Road. We then walked along the New England Highway for a while, stopping at a petrol station. The station had a hitching rail, so I tied Lucky to the rail and went inside for a cold drink. I had a chat with the owners and a few customers and they donated some batteries for my GPS. The owners Googled us and took our photos. From there we continued walking uphill. We took a break at the top of one of the hills. It was hard walking along the Highway on the grass. I tried the bitumen but then Lucky wanted to follow me. When a car came along I had to pull him off the bitumen and down the embankment to the grass. Because of the heat, uphill climb and constant tug of war with Lucky, I became exhausted. We finally arrived at our turnoff and walked down Lipps Road, a very long road and came to the end. I waved down a Ute and asked the driver if he knew Linda. He said 'no' but that we could use his house phone. So we walked to his place and phoned. I found our destination was on Reg Lipps Road. I was so tired that Brian said I could rest and have a drink and some cookies before I walked to Linda's. Brian's wife and son came home and we went over the maps and they found a place for me to stay the next night. They arranged it for us at Kathy's in Wyreema. Brian offered us to stay the night but I declined as Linda was expecting us. Energized, we began running again. Lucky and Della liked it, but Della ran on the other side of the road, I think she worried Lucky might step on her. We were welcomed at Linda's and I put the packs in the barn, Lucky had his own paddock and Della was allowed in the house. Linda's mother showed me my room and helped me with my laundry. I took a shower and felt much better. I applied some ice gel on my legs, took some Nurofen and Linda's mother cooked a delicious quiche which we ate with salad. It was such a beautiful view from Linda's window and the sky looked grey. Lucky behaved himself while I loaded him up, probably because I short tied him. Della actually ate 2 bowls of food for breakfast. I was surprised as she usually only eats half a bowl. Linda's mother waved goodbye and her horses came up to the fence to say goodbye and have a sticky beak at Lucky and his pack.

It was raining softly, which felt quite refreshing and helped cool things down. The route Brian had made for us was a pleasant quiet walk - only a few cars passed us on the dirt road. I became a little lost in Greenmount but I pulled out the GPS and we were soon on the correct path again. I had tired of the tug-of-war with Lucky and tied his lead-rope to Della's collar. Della followed me and Lucky came along behind Della. It worked, until Lucky realised that he could stop and eat grass since Della wasn't strong enough to pull him along. He became obsessed with wanting to graze, even though he'd had biscuits of hay and grain the previous night, so I had to go back and retrieve him. We had a huge 27 kilometres walk planned and my legs were already aching. Della chased a rabbit and a fox along that road - it was nice to see live wildlife instead of the usual road kill. Eighteen kilometres from our start, we stopped in Cambooya. A lovely woman came out of the house and invited us to stop for a chat. I was about ready to keel over, so agreed, only too happy to have a seat. With my legs throbbing, I tied Lucky to the trampoline, tied Della to the porch to keep her away from the house dog, and sat on a chair at the table. Josie introduced me to her children and offered water, lemonade, and cookies. Whilst her daughter gave Lucky a bucket of water and a biscuit of hay, we had an enjoyable chat about her thoroughbred and how she' showed' her horse with Linda helping and giving advice. Lucky was naughty and tried to roll the pack off, but I had it on tight and he couldn't dislodge it, even though he rolled completely over it. Hah - one up on Lucky! The storm looked about ready to come down hard, so we continued along our way. Brian stopped by in a council truck and explained we didn't have much farther to go, which was good to hear. The wind blew against us and made it hard going uphill. Lucky began walking right behind me, avoiding the wind, his nose right between my shoulder blades, and I was taking the brunt of the storm. It began sprinkling with rain and I didn't care that Lucky was on the road and not on the grass. I was exhausted from fighting him all day. On the other hand, Della was doing great as usual - such a great traveling companion. We were expected at the next stop and thankfully Steve and Darren walked down the road to greet us. I gladly handed the lead rope to Darren for him to play 'tug of war' with Lucky. Going up their driveway, Darren soon realised the problem that Lucky can be when he wants to be difficult. Steve helped me unload Lucky's pack in the shed, and Darren and Steve fixed Lucky's picket line properly by splicing it. I put the double hobbles on Lucky and the picket line, just in case. Darren gave Lucky water and Lachlan and Darren both helped me brush Lucky. Della had her dinner while Steve patched up my bags with duct tape. Wonderful Kathy cooked a very good dinner. I awoke as the sky turned grey and turned on my mobile to find a text from Alison stating she wanted to drive out from the Gold Coast to visit me. I love when Russell and Alison visit, they always bring treats! Cheered up, I replied asking if she could collect Lucky's size three boots. That morning, Darren distracted Lucky with the grain while I loaded him up and Steve took pictures. Darren wanted to walk that day, but Lucky stepped on his foot. Poor Darren, I knew how that felt. Lucky had stepped on my big toe a few weeks earlier and my nail had turned black. Steve had steel cap boots on so he came along for about five kilometres and showed me the back-ways through paddocks. Leading Lucky along he walked fast. We passed a cool refrigerated vegetable vending machine, I had to take pictures. - a vending machine dispensing fresh vegetables in the middle of nowhere! I was hoping it had carrots so I could buy some for Lucky, but it only had seasonal veggies. It is definitely worth a look if you are ever in Wyreema, QLD. Kathy drove up and collected Steve and we were on our own again. We walked along a dirt road and passed a 'Correctional Facility' sign but I didn't see any prisoners outside the property which was surrounded by a barbed-wire fence. The fence may have been good at holding cows but not so successful with people - maybe they had all escaped! It began to get hot and Lucky's behavior began to be irritating, I think he knew the whip was lost and thought he could play up. He wanted to walk along the fence line in the long grass but I didn't want the bags to snag on the barbed-wire and get another hole, so it was tug of war again. I took the extra lead rope and put a knot at the end of it and swatted Lucky's rump. Finally, he started walking faster and walking where I wanted him to walk. I began to think of ways I could prevent Lucky from continually stopping to eat grass. I took the spare lead rope and hooked it on his halter and short tied it to his saddle. So Lucky could only lower his head to his knees. *Wow,* I thought *why hadn't I thought of this weeks ago? It would have saved my arms from all the yanking and pulling.* It worked great. After a few goes at trying to eat the grass, Lucky gave up and got to the task of watching where he walked. We passed some beautiful thoroughbred and quarter horse stud farms and all the horses were interested in Lucky. He wasn't interested in them - he just kept looking at the yummy green grass and walking along. Della decided to bark and started to chase the horses, but I put a stop to that quick. I told Della 'no chasing horses, only cows, rabbits, and things I tell you to chase'. Della tried to get on my good side, but I stayed mad at her for a good five minutes, to show I was serious. Then I forgave her and told her she was being good. Della's tail started wagging again and she moved into her usual walking spot, just ahead of Lucky.

When we arrived in Biddeston we all needed a rest. I was really tired and could barely walk as we had travelled over 20 kilometres that day. A man came out of a house offering Lucky and Della water. Then, thoughtful Russell and Alison showed up with lots of wonderful gifts! Lucky's boots, carrots, apples, cookies, nut bars, poppers, and dog food. (I thought 'they'd bought half of Woolies'). Lucky ate four kilos of carrots, Della had a tray of wet dog food, I had cookies, Poppers, and a glass of cold soft-drink. Alison joined us for our walk to the end of town and called Russell to pick her up because she had tired and I was turning onto Toowoomba-Cecil Plains Road. It had been fun chatting and walking along with Alison. It was to be the last time we saw them till we returned from our trip.

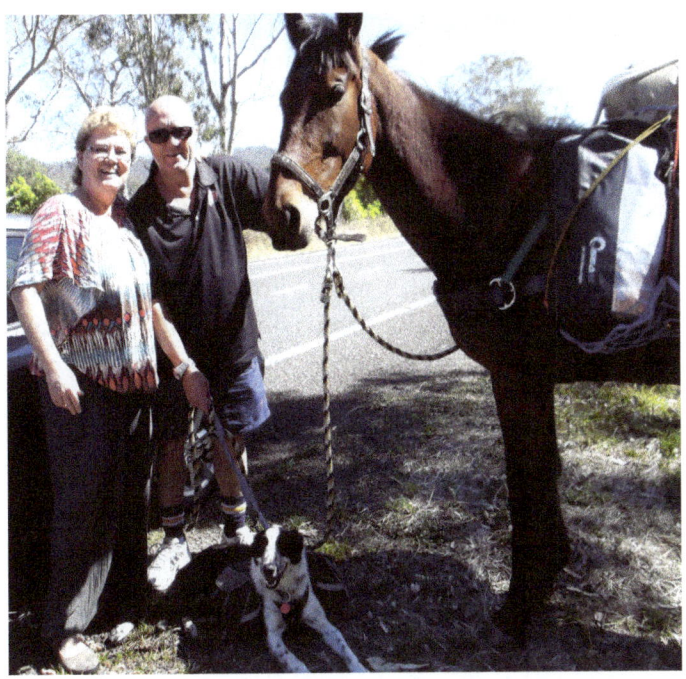

Russell and Alison Ratford with Lucky and Della

I started to get very sore feet and the last few kilometres didn't go well. I thought my feet must be bleeding again because that's what they felt like when they bled. My legs started feeling weird and stopped working properly and I thought I was going to keel over. I draped my arm over Lucky's neck to help support my weight and he continued walking, carrying my weight. After a few minutes the spasms went away and I was able to move my legs myself. I finally made it to John Riley's driveway and it looked like his house was one kilometre from the road… uphill. I managed to make it up to the house. He has some really pretty horses and they all pranced around for Lucky. Lucky didn't really care. All he wanted was to be relieved of his pack, roll in the grass and eat. We had walked for seven and a half hours and covered 34 1/2 kilometres that day. John took Lucky to the stables and I laid down on the grass to rest. Eventually, I found the energy to unload Lucky and Della. We put Lucky in the paddock and fed Della dinner and dropped off my bags. Then I tottered to the house for a welcomed soak in a bubble bath. Refreshed, I was invited to the local pub for dinner. John was friendly and talked a lot, introducing me to everyone. I met a funny, lively cowboy, who told me about buying a stockman's map that would have all the watering holes across the Northern Territory. He confirmed my intended trip was possible since he himself had been that route as a drover…encouraging news. He explained I would need a riding horse besides Lucky as my pack-horse. We talked about a buggy, but he said a buggy would be costly and a riding horse would be more flexible and easier to get to the water bores. This cowboy told me he would visit John's after work, the next day, to have another talk, as John suggested I had a rest day at his place.

I went up to the house for breakfast. John had put my clothes in the wash and I hung them up on the line to dry, before hopping on his four- wheel quad bike to show me around his property and check out his horses. He had three foals that were so cute, however, the mares chased Della away from them. I fed Lucky hay because he wasn't eating the mullet John had given him in the morning. Later that afternoon, Lorelle, Heidi and her children Bree and Trea, drove to John's house with lunch. It was great seeing them again, and doing a tour of John's homestead. We found Della was being chased by John's Welsh Cob horses. Della wanted to follow us but ended up being surrounded and I carried her out of the paddock, afraid the mares would trample her. They looked pretty determined to get Della but were just protecting their foals. Heidi had brought bags of grain and hay for Lucky. Heidi was the most thoughtful and wonderful person and I so appreciated everything she has done for us. I saddled Lucky because I was going to have the cowboy from the pub ride him. I thought this would be a good opportunity to give Lucky a ride with someone experienced in the saddle.

Chapter Two

Choco-chip

When the guy from the bar pulled up in a ute, with two horses in a float, I told him I was thinking about riding Lucky the next day. I wanted him to test Lucky by sitting on the pack saddle. Whilst he agreed, he suggested one of his geldings would be a good riding horse for me and unloaded Choco-chip. A sturdy brown and white pony with a messy mane and tail, he stood thirteen hands high. Part quarter horse, palomino, and stock horse he was six years old, small and cute and had just been shod. Unsure about having a horse with iron shoes, I realized I couldn't afford to be picky especially since this was a loan. With Lucky in tow, the cowboy rode around for a while but I noticed Lucky seemed unsure of this new situation. We three, Lucky, Della and myself, had been together for so long, anyone new was a bit daunting for him. Lucky did pretty well though and behaved. John arrived as it was time to leave for dinner at his friends' house. After settling the horses in the stable, the guy took his saddle and reins saying he would drop off replacements but leave me with a saddle, blanket and hobble. I thanked him profusely and he agreed to collect

Choco-chip in Roma and drove off. I was in shock that a stranger would loan me a horse when I didn't even know his name – *it could be a title to a country western song*! Once I was in John's car I asked him the man's name as I didn't remember and found John had forgotten too, so we stopped at the local pub. John went inside to ask the bartender and learned the very generous man's name was Craig Morris. I spent the evening with John at his mates' house, Denni Darr and his wife. They were both very friendly and we had a lovely meal - the dessert was just delicious. Returning to John's I collected my things from his house and took them to the gooseneck (a horse-trailer with a sleeping compartment) and assembled my bed. My 5:30 am alarm woke me and I quickly readied myself and went to the stables where I found John looking at my gear. He offered to take my supplies to the Woolshed. He took the big bags so Lucky's pack was quite light. I saddled Choco-Chip, deciding to call him 'Chockie'. He seemed so short compared to Lucky but he stood well while being saddled. Astride him, I took off with Lucky beside me and circled a few times to get them used to each other. Della seemed bewildered seeing me on top of a horse but she followed, keeping her distance. John helped us across the street and we continued along to get our previously arranged picture taken at the pub for the local newspaper. I managed to get both of the horses trotting with Della running alongside without her pack, since Lucky was carrying everything. I didn't know how fast we would be traveling and worried we would wear her out but her tail continued to wag, telling me she enjoyed our walks. Chockie slowed down after the first hour of riding so I climbed down and walked. He was easy to lead and didn't stop to eat the grass along the way. Since he was tied-up short to his saddle, Lucky couldn't eat the grass either and this made the walking pleasant, especially on the back roads. Previously, Lucky never wanted to walk close to me but being tied to Chockie, he kept trying to head him off and walk right behind me trying to keep his head on my shoulder. I climbed back on Chockie and Lucky walked so close that he bumped my right knee. I tried to push Lucky away with my hand and my knee became quite sore. As we walked through the cotton growing alongside the road, the white balls looked like a pillow had exploded. I applied sunscreen and put the tube into the netting on Lucky's pack saddle with my seven-inch knife (that had been banging against my back) but with our little trots, both items must have fallen out along West Prairie Creek Road. While I was riding I spotted a huge black snake in the grass. Fortunately both of the horses were jostling each other so they didn't notice. Della walked ahead, far away from the arguing horses, as the snake slithered into a hole. Arriving at the Jondaryn Woolshed, it looked like there would be a huge storm. Overhead, the dark clouds were thick as the rain starting spitting and I checked into the Shearer's Quarters. John arrived and helped unload as I placed the supplies in the stable and put both horses to graze in the paddock. After tying Della up outside my bunk door I jumped into John's ute to head for Toowoomba where we shopped for Choco-chip's tack and the Queensland Stockman's Route and Water Points Map. I expressed my deep gratitude to John for all his help as he returned me to the Woolshed. Back at the paddock I brushed both horses and had to cut most of Chockie's tail off, (coated as it was in mud and poo), as well as the hard caked mud-covered hair off the bottom of his legs. I gave Lucky's tail a trim too, so Chockie wouldn't feel bad about having a short tail. I tried to look at Chockie's shod hooves, but he was really sensitive and wouldn't let me clean them. I lifted Lucky's hooves in front of him and showed him that I cleaned them out with the hook pick and brush, and then tried Chockie again but he wasn't having any of it. I left him be, but from what I could see Chockie's hooves looked in a bad state. I put the grain filled nose bag on Lucky then tied Chockie up with his grain on the ground. Well Lucky was having none of sharing his grain even though greedy Lucky couldn't eat Chockie's grain because he had his nose bag on. As soon as my back was turned, I heard Lucky go after Chockie who broke the lead-rope to get away. Lucky was being mean to the little pony. It was just jealousy. I untied the lead-rope and hit Lucky on the rump, chasing him away, encouraging Chockie back and stood watch over him and kept the lead-rope in my hand, swinging it around whenever Lucky got too close. The little pony took forever to eat - he was probably nervous, looking over his shoulder at Lucky. After Chockie finished, I took Lucky's nose bag off and left the horses in the paddock. I sorted out the supplies for the next day and filled the water bottles, fixed the lead-rope and headed for a shower. Before going to bed, with a sigh, I threw my favourite dirty torn jeans into the trash.

When I climbed out of bed at 6am the next morning, it felt cold. I carried my gear to the stables and then filled up the nose bag and Lucky followed me right into the arena without a lead-rope. I'd put Lucky's halter on Chockie last night so I could tie him up while being fed and left it on so it would be easier to catch him in the morning. (Lucky just follows me around, especially if I have that nose-bag in hand.) Chockie came over to investigate the nose-bag I'd left it on the ground. I put him in a stall, grabbed some rope from my bag, and made him a rope halter. Putting Lucky's halter back on him, I saddled them both - Lucky with the pack saddle and Chockie with the riding saddle and the small saddle bags. Della was saddled up last. Then I tied them all up to the hitching rail before looking for a Woolshed employee. I found a few having morning tea at the damper shed and gave them the bag containing Craig Morris's saddle blanket and spurs. I explained he would be stopping by to pick them up. We headed off, me riding Chockie and leading Lucky with Della in front. It was a short walk to Jondorayn but once in the town, I dismounted and walked Chockie because he was frightened of everything. He refused to walk on the concrete sidewalk until I walked on it first. We then stopped at a creek and Lucky and Della had a drink. Chockie didn't want one. A Rottweiler dog came running across the street barking at us and I was afraid I would lose Chockie for good. I held on tight to his reins, but the dog went for Della who did her usual running away with her tail between her legs and the owner of the dog came running and yelling. The owner caught his dog, Della came back unharmed and I still had the horses so all was well. When we came to the highway, I walked them all on foot. I tried to ride Chockie but he was so slow, I returned to alternate walking and riding. I felt lazy in the saddle and I wanted to give my legs a stretch. I had a feeling we moved faster when we just walked. At the end of the day we were averaging 4.4 kilometres an hour which was .2 slower than when it was just three of us walking. So adding another horse wasn't making us travel faster, but since it was less tiring for me, we could travel for longer and could carry more things. As I walked the horses along the dirt road, Denni Darr stopped by. He looked at Chockie's hooves and declared they wouldn't last till Roma. Since he was a farrier, he offered to replace them right there. He pulled out his farrier gear and changed Chockie's shoes in the middle of the dirt road. There was no traffic on this road at all; not one car came along while he was working. I wasn't happy about shoeing the horse (I like the 'bare-foot' approach) but Chockie already had shoes and he wasn't my horse. I would have removed the shoes, give him a few days in a paddock to get used to his bare feet, then put him in 'Easy Boots' for the trip. However, Chockie was on loan, so I held onto his reins and watched Denni replace his front shoes. Chockie stood patiently and didn't appear to feel pain as the nails were driven into his hoof whilst I was cringing at every clang of the hammer. I think I was more affected then Chockie. I thanked Denni as he left and told him I'd have a drink for him at the Bowenville pub. Astride Chockie, we headed toward Bowenville. I tied up the horse to the front of the pub and had a brief chat with the owner who offered to keep the horses in his backyard and have me camp there for the night. Denni Darr arrived to help unload the horses so I left the horses in the green grassy backyard. Inside for a couple of glasses of wine and a chat with the farrier and owner, I ate a couple of bags of chips and returned to the horses. Outside I put leather polish on the saddle while Denni made a proper rope halter for Chockie as the one I'd made earlier kept falling off his nose. Before he left, I thanked Denni, so nice and helpful, for everything – I hoped I'd meet more people like him. I fed Della, did a load of laundry, put up the swag, took a shower, tied the horses up separately and fed them grain. Craig Morris arrived to check on his horse, Choco-chip, and he gave me a piece of paper with his name and phone number. He checked Chockie over but wasn't happy about the short tail, until I explained that it was too hard to get it cleaned. I told him about the new shoes, showed him the new gear, and explained that his old gear was at the Woolshed for collection. Saying goodbye, I went into the pub for a fish and chips dinner and gave most of the chips to Della. The dessert was beautiful and I went straight to bed after dinner.

I woke early, as I wanted to get to Dalby in time to go to the 'opportunity' shop and buy a cheap pair of jeans, since I only had one pair to wear. The day was still so the flies were all over us and I reached over and brushed them off Lucky's face when I was riding. We stopped at a creek for a drink, before walking Blaxand Road. After another break, whilst giving Della water from my water bottle, Chockie accidentally stepped on Della's rear foot. She yelped and Chockie took off but, since he was tied to Lucky who was eating grass, Chockie didn't get anywhere. I looked at Della's foot and it was bleeding - I used an alcohol swab from my medical supplies and watched Della walk. She wasn't limping and we were almost at the Showground so I didn't bandage it. I decided that if I saw it bleeding and she looked sore, I would bandage it. I kept a close eye on her walking and 27 kilometres later we reached Dalby Showground. Chockie started acting up as soon as we were in town. He shied away from everything so I dismounted and lead Chockie and tied Lucky to the back. He didn't jump as easily. Della and I took the lead walking through Dalby, a bigger town than I had expected. A man working on the front of his house offered water for the horses and Della, so I took him up on his offer. Della and Lucky drank out of the green collapsible water bucket, but Chockie refused. I tried everything I could think of but he just wouldn't. The man's name was Dick and he offered to drive up to the Showground to make sure they were open. On his return, he stopped on the road and told me which gate was open and said he would go to the council to make sure the gates remained unlocked. Later, at the Showground, Dick said that they wanted me to go register and would charge me ten dollars. He drove me to their offices and Dick paid the ten dollars for me before stopping at the OP shop. I ran in and quickly grabbed some clothing including two pairs of jeans. He dropped me off at the Showground saying he would return at 6:30am to unlock the gate. I placed the horses in hobbles so they could walk around and graze whilst I took a shower. A newspaper reporter arrived and after a chat, said he would be back in the morning to take our picture, locking the gate behind him. Dark grey clouds gathered overhead and it seemed a storm was brewing. I picked all the bindis out of Lucky's boots and the saddle pads and made up a bed in the judges' booth under the counter. I couldn't be bothered setting up the swag and folding up a wet swag next morning, getting myself wet and muddy. I cooked dinner and filled up the water bottles, organised the gear for the next day and planned my trip to Roma. Around 9pm I decided to put the horses in the paddock for the night. It was dark and I couldn't find them. I walked all around the Showground with a torch calling for Lucky and listening for the clink of their hobbles – I hadn't realised the grounds were so huge. I gave up walking around after half an hour and returned to the judging booth, listening hard for the jingle of the hobbles. When I heard it I was so happy I climbed out from under the counter and listened some more, determining which direction to take. I put my boots on, grabbed the lead-rope and found the horses asleep under a tree. I took Lucky's hobbles off and attached the rope, leading him to the paddock. The little pony didn't want to get left behind and began following in his hobbles. I was afraid he would stumble in the dark, so I let go of Lucky and took off Chockie's hobbles. Lucky had wandered away, enough for me to yell and grab the lead-rope. It had dragged along the ground and now had bindis all through it, pricking my hand. I couldn't hold the rope so I draped the rope along my shoulder. This turned out to be the wrong thing to do when wearing a fleece jumper. After I put the horses in the paddock, I had to spend the next twenty minutes picking bindis out of my jumper before I could go to sleep. I didn't bother with the rope, it was too dark and I figured I would do it in the morning. I was tired and my brain obviously wasn't working. Della slept next to me with my arm around her all night and she loved that. Before falling asleep, my last thoughts were about her, hoping she stayed safe on this walk.

I woke at 5 am, to a grey sky and started on my jumper – the bindis appeared to have multiplied and were stuck to everything. Della didn't wear her backpack today due to her injury from the previous day. I had enough grain to get to Kogan, so with the horses packed we were ready for the day. Dick arrived at 6am and told me directions to a short cut to get out of Dalby. To make it easier, he took me for a quick ride in his car to show me. When we arrived back at the Showground, the newspaper bloke was there to take Della's picture then headed following Dick's directions. I found a four-wheel drive trek that was off the highway, and took it (because Chockie had begun to act up) ending up on the stock route which is now the underground gas pipe-line route. It was a very hot and sunny day. The horses were too busy arguing with each other to notice, but I saw a black snake with a red belly. The snake didn't move - it just laid there and flicked its tongue out. Della was way ahead chasing kangaroos so I held my breath and guided Chockie round it and Lucky followed. By 11am we had passed three dried up streams and I was worried about Della. She'd been running around chasing animals we'd come across, rolling in the dirt and panting away. I knew she needed water so I stopped at the next house we came across. The owners were very nice and Della drank out of the water trough. I tied up the horses to the trough too. Invited inside, we used a tea bag that John Riley had given me and had a 'cuppa' and took their advice on the road ahead. I walked the horses down their driveway before mounting. I tried walking - I enjoyed walking and looked forward to a nice road for me to walk along - but it was hard in the long grass. I had been walking too slowly and the horses were fighting over who would be closest to me. I didn't enjoy their nose-blowing on each side of my face. It was just easier to ride although I felt lazy and unfit in the saddle. Lucky notified me the lead-rope had broken once again by stopping and eating grass. I fixed it with the pliers in my bag but we had to stop a few times anyway, under a tree, for shade. The lunchtime heat became overwhelming and without a breeze, the flies descended. I went to the bush toilet and it was gross, the flies smothered me. Attracted to moisture, they kept going in our eyes and up our noses. It was horrible trying to keep them away. Della rolled on her back and covered herself in dirt and when we came to the

Condamine River, Della, who loves swimming, went in to cool off. The river was so low she couldn't swim properly but the horses walked through it. At about 3pm we came upon a little dam and the horses trotted over for a drink and sunk up to their knees in the mud. Lucky didn't lose his boots but I had a massive cleaning job. We stopped at a house and asked if we could camp but they explained there was a creek 100 meters away down a dirt road with a grassy camping area, which happened to be the creek I was looking for. When we arrived there, I noted that we had walked 32 kilometres that day. Della went swimming whilst I unloaded quickly and put the horses in hobbles, cleaning Lucky's boots. I fixed the broken lead-rope again, and set up the swag. I started cooking my dinner and Lucky came snooping along so I put him on the picket line. Lucky stuck his nose in my swag, in all my bags, in my food container, in my hat, and almost burnt his nose by sticking it in the boiling water! Chockie didn't seem to like Lucky being out of his sight so I left Chockie in hobbles. Then I began to worry and tied Chockie to a tree. I moved him from tree to tree throughout the night, so he could eat the grass. The mozzies were bad by the creek so they added to the day's irritations - flies, heat, and broken lead-ropes. When we had a breeze it was so much better, the flies went away and it just seemed cooler. I had to get buckets of water from the creek next morning because the horses didn't like going down the embankment into the mud. After feeding them the last of the grain, I loaded them and had everything ready to go when I decided to use the bush toilet before we hit the road. I discovered that I had started my monthly cycle and my tampons were in the pack on Lucky, so I made a bush tampon out of toilet paper.

Instructions on making bush tampons:
- Use only 3 squares
- Fold lengthwise in half
- Roll as tightly as possible
- Insert
- You may have to dig pieces out, so make sure you have soap and water handy.
- Always remove before going pee.

It's messy but it works. I finally figured it out on my 3rd bush tampon for the day.

What not to do when making bush tampons:
- Don't use more than 3 squares.
- Don't fold after rolling. Folding lengthwise is always first

All those packing manuals and books and they never mention these things. Always keep at least 2 tampons in your waist pack, even if you know you're not going to start, cause with bad luck like me, you will start early.

Several people stopped to take our picture but we had lost the wonderful open clear stock route as the electric and mining companies had fenced it off with padlocked gates. We were forced to walk alongside a very busy gravel-lined road. Lucky hated walking on the gravel and I felt so sorry for him. I decided to put rear shoes on him for the next day putting the new shoes on his front feet and the old shoes on his back hooves. We walked 24 kilometres and it was hard going, due to the gravel on the side of the road. I had to carry buckets of water for the horses from the first creek but thankfully the horses could walk to the second. Della had a good day and was exhausted having had swims in both creeks and chasing two large lizards up trees. Again, it began getting very hot around noon. I began to think we may have to start traveling in the morning and evening, as the middle of the day was too hot. We arrived at the Kogan Hotel and the owners, a very lovely couple, made us feel very welcome. Della and I stayed inside and had lunch at the bar. Lucky and Chockie stayed next door in a grassy paddock belonging to one of the pub's patrons and we stored the supplies in a container. I had to carry five gallon buckets of water to the paddock five times throughout the day and night - horses drink a lot of water! I washed my clothes in the shower and relaxed before sorting the supplies. Andy, a local, came to the pub with a present of a bag of working horse grain for me. I thanked him and had a few glasses of wine and dinner, chatting to the friendly locals. It was a good night and I drifted off to sleep wishing everyday would end up in a pub with drinks.

I woke up at 4:45am and was loaded up and on the road by 6 - the earliest time ever. I knew we had a big day ahead of us. Thankfully, the horses behaved and ate their grain while I packed them. Lucky wore four boots but walked slowly with Choco-chip pulling him along. Chockie behaved well except for his problem with road trash, walking round everything - he seemed to think everything's out to get him. Sometimes he forgot who Della was and stopped and stared. Just so silly but at least he moves along at a fast walk unlike Lucky, who has long legs and could easily keep up, but slowly plods along. I took turns pulling Lucky along, then my arm became sore, and I let Chockie pull him. I had thought his sluggishness was due to bare rear hooves and the gravel causing him to be slow but on a better road and wearing all four boots he didn't walk any faster. Della had a great day with no pack. She went swimming, chased wallabies and sniffed everything. I think she walks three times the distance we do because she is always chasing, or running ahead, then running back. Della gets so much exercise, when we get to camp she always takes a big sleep before eating her dinner. Many road-trains flashed by and one of them hit a wallaby on the road ahead. As we walked past, I saw the wallaby lift its head. I felt horrible. I tied up the horses, walked onto the road and picked it up, laying it down on grass at the side of the road. Its tail had been run over and broken, but it's legs looked fine. I hope it recovered. I felt so sad and Della could tell that the wallaby was in pain and stayed away. Della wouldn't chase an injured wallaby; she only likes chasing the fast ones she can't catch. She wouldn't know what to do if she caught one. Now thinking of all the road-kill makes me sad and upset. These animals crawl to the side of the road in pain and die, just like this wallaby had been trying to do. I've seen so much road-kill and wish it wouldn't happen. This day I'd seen some twenty animals on the side of the road. I couldn't hit an animal. In the past, I've almost run into a ditch, swerving to avoid hitting a turtle on the road when I was driving. Lucky and Della drank from every creek we passed but Chockie just wasn't interested. He didn't drink from the water bucket at all - maybe he doesn't get as thirsty as Lucky and Della. I know Della becomes thirsty especially with all her running around. The sky was overcast and windy, so we didn't have a fly problem. We walked for eight hours, doing a total of 41.2 kilometres. I rode for most of the day and was very sore. I started walking towards the end of the day as I needed to stretch my legs and rest my bum. We averaged 5.1 kilometres an hour. We only took one hour total rest break and it was a great days walk. The horses ate a great deal of grain that evening. It began raining so I headed off the dirt path and went to the end where there was a creek and a campsite with a table, a fire pit and a railing down to the creek. I unloaded quickly, and spread the tarp over everything. Della crawled underneath whilst I sorted out the horses. I placed Lucky on the picket line and Chockie in hobbles hoping he was there in the morning and hadn't run off. We were far enough from the roadway that I did not have to worry about him walking on the road. I don't think he would attempt to go down the steep embankment to the creek with hobbles on - he wouldn't go near it without hobbles. I don't understand why Chockie likes Lucky so much as he is so mean and demanding, wanting his water and food first. I have to separate them so Lucky doesn't push Chockie away. In the morning it was so overcast and dark, I couldn't see properly to untie the tarp from the trees. I climbed back into the swag for fifteen minutes until the sun came up… just enough through the clouds so I could see. I packed up everything, and returned to where the horses were left the night before. Lucky had managed to walk round and round his tree causing him to become tangled up, so he was not grazing. Chockie was nearby and chomping away on the grass, so I gave Lucky an extra helping of grain while I loaded him up. I noticed that Lucky had a welt on his back that looked like a blister, so I switched sides with the bags and hoped that helped. The weather was excellent, cloudy, breezy, and not hot – perfect walking weather. Lucky misbehaved and my arm became very sore so I had to get off Chockie and spank Lucky a few times until he stopped pulling on the lead-rope. It was a great scenic day, except for the mines. I noticed three very large kangaroos in the distance but Della hadn't seen them as they were too far away. Enjoying the day, I made a promise to myself that I will not stress about how long this trip took. I couldn't change the fact that it was going to take a long time. I felt I should enjoy every day of the journey and stop worrying about how far and fast I'm going.

WEEK 5

It was Sunday and I thought it would be a slow day but the road was so busy with road-trains and trucks going back and forth. We passed lots of water, due to the fact that it rained the previous night. Lucky and Della drank at every opportunity, whilst Choco-chip only had a few drinks. I began to think that he doesn't need as much water as the other two. Della started limping, although she kept up and still chased animals and ran around. I decided to take her to the vet in Roma. I actually had the horses up to a trot, which was good especially as I didn't think Lucky could walk faster than a walk.

Lucky, Della, Choco-chip and I

We arrived in Condamine and asked a few people where the Showground were and no one knew. I went into the pub and an old bloke said it was three kilometres back on the road going north. Well I was tired, it was getting hot, and I didn't want to backtrack, so I thought *bugger it I'll camp by the river, next to the pub.* I unloaded and hobbled the horses, put Lucky on the picket line because he started wandering away, before going into the pub and having a bag of chips and a glass of wine. I met the postal bloke and we checked my intended route. He thought I should stick to the highway but it's twenty-seven kilometers longer that way and I wanted to go down a quiet dirt road through the forest, which I hoped would be cooler and shadier. I walked to the store but it shut at 1pm on Sundays. It opened again at 6am, so I decided to return there in the morning and pick up supplies. The flies were really bad so I needed to buy netting for my hat in Roma. I really hated those flies, they landed on everything, one even went up my nose and I had to blow it out. I hauled up the first bucket of water from the steep embankment for the horses before thinking better of it and brought them water from the tap at the back of the pub. The next time I watered them I just led them up to the back of the pub to fill their bucket, then I didn't have to carry it all the way to the campsite. Later in the pub for tea, I documented all the watering spots in my book. I mapped it out from the Google maps on my iPad. I hadn't finished my food, so I had it put in a box for Della who gobbled it up right away - she had been eating a lot lately. I untangled Lucky and put his picket line around another tree, then found Chockie and tied him to a tree. He'd been too far away and I was worried he might cross the street thinking I may have to get up again in the middle of the night and sort him out. My alarm went off in the morning and I lay there for another ten minutes. It was just so dark outside - hard to see anything at all. Lucky was very naughty while putting his boots on, so I took his nose-bag away but when he cooperated I gave him his grain sack back. Meanwhile Choco-chip ate his grain before wandering off to eat grass. After I finished with Lucky I walked him to the back of the pub to water him and Chockie came running, thinking he was being left behind. I saddled Chockie, gave all three water and we rode to the store. It was tiny and didn't have dog food. I had fed Della all her food the night before so I ended up buying her two frozen meat pies, frozen mince, four bags of beef jerky, and a can of beef stew. I would have bought more but I cleaned out the store. It cost $55.00 - the can of beef stew was $6.00 and the beef jerky $5.80 a bag. I hoped it would last four days but if she ate it all, I'd give her some of my food. To top it all, I forgot to get myself some snack bars. We headed off over the bridge and continued down Roma-Condamine Road - a lovely scenic ride and we picked up the stock/gas-pipe route. Free of road-kill, this route was really pleasant and I was able to smell their perfume as we passed trees in flower. We overtook a live echidna and I told Della 'NO' and she just looked and walked around it as it curled up into a cute ball. It was good to see a live one instead of the dead ones on the road. Colourful birds flew around us as we travelled the 35 kilometres. We came across a lake and I took the horses down to the water. I led Lucky and Chockie followed along but went knee-deep in the muddy lake and did a roll with his saddle on. I yelled and it startled him so that he stood back up but I could tell he was going to finish the roll, so I grabbed Lucky and walked away. It worked, he didn't want to be left behind, and ran out of the lake to follow us. I had to tie Chockie up and wash the mess off the saddle and bags. It was so hot in the afternoon so we took a few breaks at the streams and creeks for water, and to allow the horses to eat some grass. On one break, I noticed flies around the shopping bag, so I opened it and discovered that the mince had a hole in the plastic, attracting the flies. I fed the mince to Della who ate the whole thing. At the next creek I took off my bra and dipped it in the water before putting it back on so I felt really refreshed. I took buckets of water and dumped them over the horses' rears and fronts. Della was already swimming of course – she's so easy to care for, the horses are the problem. I really should have bought a big dog that could carry our stuff, then I wouldn't have needed horses. After our eight hours walk we arrived at Moraby Creek and set up camp. It was a lovely spot, right on the stock route, but there was no time to sit around with so much to do. After feeding and watering the horses, I placed Lucky on the picket line, put healing ointment on his nose, hobbled Chockie, set up the swag, organised the next days water, cooked and ate food, washed dishes and clothes, untangled Lucky's picket line, brushed horses, and checked all three for ticks. By the time I climbed into my swag, the sun had set. Then I had to update my diary and look over the route we were to take the following day. Exhausted, with the thought that *'this feels like a full time job'* I closed my eyes thinking *at least it's doing something I love and for a good cause*. The next day, Chockie stepped on my foot as I saddled him. It hurt so much, bent over with pain, I had to wait until it subsided before I could finish. Eventually, we set off following the stock / gas pipe-line route. We passed the Jackson turn-off, because the postman at the Condamine Hotel had told me it was a bitumen road. By the time I realised that was our turn-off, we had gone too far to go back so we continued along the Roma-

Condamine Road. We had lost the stock route so we had to go back to the road. It was a quiet road but there was the smell of road kill and those hated flies everywhere. Two of the flies went up my nose... disgusting. I noticed that Della was getting thinner and it worried me. *When I get to Roma I'm going to talk to the vet.* A guy stopped and had a chat. He filled up my water bottles with his cold fresh water and it was so good! He said that we could camp at Yuleba Creek - there was an abandoned schoolhouse next to the creek. So we made our way there to an outdoor lunch area, where Della and I slept. For once, I didn't have to put up the swag. Except for Chockie, we unloaded, and rode down to the creek. I gathered water for the horses, took off my shirt and jeans and put my water shoes on. I waded into the creek for a bath and the water was so cold it gave me goosebumps. I climbed out, soaped myself up and jumped back in to rinse off. After I toweled dry and put my shirt and jeans on, I felt so refreshed. It had been too long since I had a shower/bath. I walked the horses back to the lunch area and picketed Lucky, putting Chockie in hobbles on the fence. I found a water tap, but the water came out white and fizzy. I made Della rice with beef jerky for breakfast, and I myself apple crumble for tea with the fizzy water. I figured the water would be safe since I boiled it. Della had beef stew for dinner and half of the rice with beef jerky. I saved a bowl of the beef jerky rice for her breakfast. A guy stopped by and told me about a good spot to camp the next day, at a station called Banoona. He explained the tap had bore water with soda in it and confirmed I wouldn't die from drinking it. I replied that I'd used it to make dinner, saving my drinking water for the day. I filled up my empty bottles with the white fizzy bore water, thinking it would be better than nothing. He returned later with two large Mount Franklin bottles of waters for which I thanked him. Now I had sufficient water for the next day. It was good to be able to sleep next to Della all night and cuddle her. She felt all bones and I was very worried. During the day she acted happy and loved chasing wallabies and had lots of energy. During the night, Della put her head across my neck to cuddle me back, but I couldn't sleep with the pressure on my neck, so I placed her head on my shoulder. I woke when the alarm went off and rose straight away, happy that it would be easier to pack as I didn't have to fold up the swag. Lucky acted-up again with his boots, so I took him away from the grain and he behaved. After his boots were on I led him back to his grain and we were on the road at 6:30am. It was a fresh, sunny, morning. We needed to start a bit earlier than usual in order to have more traveling time during the cooler part of the day. It took us a while before we crossed the first creek. The embankment was steep with only a few water holes left, due to the drought. I tied up the horses and Della and I went down to the water. I had to fill the bucket four times, up and down that embankment. I had no rest time. However, I did take my shirt off and put it in the water and it was cool and refreshing to wear. Then I thought *what the hell*, and stuck my head in the water bucket and wet my hair - now that was very refreshing. Della went swimming while I threw sticks for her and she yelped, I was instantly worried a crocodile had gotten her when she didn't respond to my call. I remembered the locals saying that there are no crocs in the area and this water hole was way too small to have a croc big enough to eat Della. Della came out but didn't tell me what was wrong. I looked around and noticed lots of wasps so maybe she got stung by one. We headed off and didn't encounter another creek - they were all dried up – but we did pass three wild feral hogs that had been hit by traffic. That was the first time I had seen them and they looked very ugly, decomposing on the side of the road. We had a break because it was so hot and the previous guy passed again and said that we were almost at Banoona. Lucky decided go do a roll because he wanted his pack off, so break time was over and we continued on our way. We arrived at Banoona, which had many houses on the property and came upon a bloke named Peter, operating a grain machine. He said we could go to the house and talk to the owner. So I tied up the horses and told Della to stay. I finally found the correct house and Charles the owner was very friendly. He let me stay in the shearer's quarters. It had a bed, hot water, and a shower and a bathroom it was excellent! He even gave me a bag of barley for the horses and dog food for Della. I took a shower and washed my clothes in the shower…just bliss! Later I chatted with Charles about my route and he invited me to dinner at the main house. 7pm was passed my bedtime, but I wasn't going to miss a fresh hot feed. (By now I had begun to feel a bit dissatisfied with my prepackaged dried food.) Suddenly the electricity went out. I had put the kettle on for a cuppa to delay my hunger pains and figured I must have blown a fuse. I tried flipping the main switch, but nothing worked, so I gave up, collected my maps, Della's food dish and my broken swag pole and headed for the house. When I arrived Charles explained Sarah, his wife had phoned, there was a fire on Roma-Condamine Road and it had burnt an electricity pole - the house electricity was out too. Charles said he would fix my swag pole in the morning and drop it off to me while I travelled along the next day. Sarah arrived home and started cooking dinner on the gas stove and I had a glass of wine while waiting. We had fish, salad, and mashed potatoes. I could have eaten a whole plate of mashed potatoes on my own. We had a good chat about things; they made a vet appointment for me on Saturday and I went off to bed. I was worried about Della, so I got up many times throughout the night to make sure she drank water and ate her dog food. The next day it was just so cold I didn't get out of bed till 5:10am. I made a Mocha for breakfast, while putting Lucky's boots on, I noticed his rear hooves had bled and scabbed over, so I didn't put boots on his back hooves. I smothered ointment on his heels and hoped that helped. *Now the vet needs to look at Della and Lucky.* We were on the road by 6:30am. Lucky kept whinnying goodbye to the other horses for quite a while. All the cows in the wheat field stopped eating to stare, it made me laugh, thinking we had such a captivated audience. This day was the first time I saw an emu, possum, and hare as road kill. I walked for quite a time because the side of the road was level and easy to walk on. I had a bit of problem with Lucky wanting to go slow, not knowing if it was due to his hooves. We were walking on grass for most of the day, so it should have been fine for him. I think he just didn't like the heavy load ...he was now carrying a 20 kilo grain sack – but the grain went down so quickly, it wouldn't be that heavy for long. His total load had been about 50 kilos and now it was 70 kilos and I think he just didn't approve. Charles stopped by in his car, telling me he had fixed my swag pole, so I didn't have to buy a new one. It was so kind of him to do that for me. We had stopped at two creeks today for water. It was still early and cool when we came to the first creek. I had to go down with the bucket but the horses weren't very thirsty. At the next creek they were able to go and help themselves. I took them down one at a time though, because I didn't trust Chocochip not to roll in the mud. We passed a road crew and the traffic controller emptied four water bottles into the bucket, so Della drank first, Chockie didn't want any, and Lucky finished it off. I poured the remainder of the water on Chockie to help cool him off. We passed by the fire area, where there were still smouldering fire spots, lots of smoke and a sign out that said 'smoke hazard'. I was a bit worried that the fire would start again. It became very hot and we arrived at a rest area that had a water tank. I put the horses under the shade and filled up the water bucket, but they didn't seem interested. I began to worry that they were overheated, so I dumped a few buckets of cold water on the horses and Della. My shirt came off and went into the bucket, so did my hair - I felt so much better with a wet shirt and wet hair. Della drank from the water then crawled under the picnic table and went to sleep. The horses began to go to fall asleep as well so I offered them some extra grain to boost their energy levels. And off we went again. Charles stopped by on his way home from town where he'd picked up a motor bike that was now lying in the back of his ute. I mentioned the heat and how I must start earlier, because it was just too hot for the horses and Della, although she doesn't carry her bag anymore she still felt the heat. We finally arrived at Blythe Creek, our intended camp. Chockie braved the embankment and mud to get water. Lucky tried but chickened out so I had to go down with the bucket and fill it for him. It would have been easy if the creeks were all flowing - the horses could have got their own water. Most of the streams we passed this day were dry and empty. I hated the drought for making the creeks and streams so low. The effects of the drought could also be seen in the local wildlife and landscape. Australia can be such a harsh yet beautiful country at times. With Lucky on the picket line I trusted Chockie not to run off. I just hoped Chockie didn't try to go for water with his hobbles on as he would most probable get stuck in the mud. There was no chance that he could drown as there is not enough water in the mud-hole - now passing for a creek. My swag was actually set up in the riverbed…that's how dry it was. I hoped it rained soon, because the countryside desperately needed it. The smoke woke me at 2am and I worried the fire had started again. It was hard to fall back to sleep because I felt excited about the night start and worried about the smoke and fire but I made myself go back to sleep till 3:30am. It seemed I had just fallen asleep when the alarm went off. Half awake, it took me two hours to load up - packing camp is hard, whilst trying to hold a flashlight. I also had problems with my scoliosis, I took three Neurofen tablets to ease the pain. I decided that when we arrived in Roma I would buy a headlamp and visit a Physio about my back and neck problems. The horses behaved - they fell asleep after eating their grain. By the time the sky turned grey, we were on the road. It was a later start than I had planned, but I needed to see how I felt. Riding was very painful so I tried walking for a while, but I couldn't walk fast due to my back pain. I was in a rock and a hard place you might say. We came to the first rest area hoping for water but there was none in the tank. A man pulled up in his ute and accused me of cutting his dogs loose from a tree. I told him that I didn't know what he was talking about. He bellowed that, since I was from PETA, I would be the only person to do that. I told him I hadn't let his dogs loose. He said his dogs had been tied to the tree for five months and no one had cut them down before. I replied I hadn't seen any dogs and I wasn't on anyone's property. He didn't believe me and continued to accuse me. It was difficult to keep my calm, however I needed to conserve my energy for the days walk. Instead, I politely asked him why he tied his dogs to a tree for five months and he replied that the dogs were dead and that he killed the two dingos and hung them from the tree on the side of the highway. I asked him why and he answered 'so people would know I killed the dingos'. I told him that I would not climb a tree to cut down two rotten smelly fly-infested dead dogs. I feel sorry for dingos, but me cutting them down isn't going to do anything to help them. He said that Charles had told him I was from PETA so I would be the only person in the area to do that. I suggested to him that maybe they fell down, if they had been hanging for five months - maybe the rope broke and they fell. I gave up trying to clear my name and he continued, bragging about how he killed fifty feral pigs. I like to refer to people such as this man as simply a wanker. Depressed, I left the rest area and had a big cry that someone I didn't even know had accused me of something that I didn't do. *I'm on a charity walk, my back and neck hurts so much, and just because I love animals I get treated like crap.* I'd already decided that Roma wasn't going to be a pleasant place. Because I was in pain and upset, I wasn't paying attention as I usually do, so when Chockie spooked over a sign, I fell off the saddle and was dragged along the gravel and bindis, before being trampled by hooves. In the two seconds before I blacked out, I realised that this could be how I met my death. I woke up, aware I was alive but couldn't see very well - everything was blurred. I lay on my side with Della licking my face and Lucky's lead rope two inches away.

I picked myself up off the ground by using Lucky's leg and cautiously assessed the damage. I was in pain but, amazingly, my back felt better. I guess it must have 'cracked', which is what I had needed. I grabbed onto Lucky's leg to fully pull myself up as my legs weren't working properly. Chockie was standing in the middle of Roma-Condamine Road and walked over to us - thankfully I didn't have to chase him. Fortunately I had been wearing my drover jacket so my arms weren't cut. My belt had broken and my jeans and underwear had bindis all over them, so I had to brush and pick them off...I didn't feel great but no bones seemed broken.

I climbed back on Chockie and this time kept my full attention on him. When we arrived at Roma we passed a creek and we all had a drink. Della went into the water for her usual cool down. At the Showground I had a chat about my injuries with the caretaker and he told me the doctor's address. Ben, from the newspaper, showed up to do an interview and I told him I wasn't feeling good, explaining what had happened. He took a few photos and I unloaded and dumped my stuff, had a quick shower and walked over a kilometer to the doctors' surgery. The receptionist informed me they were booked out, but I explained that I had an accident and need to see someone and she suggested the hospital. When I replied 'I'm walking, is it far?' she said she would see if she could fit me in. Crying and wanting to lie down, I sat in the lobby until finally they called me in. I started crying again and the poor foreigner lady doctor couldn't understand me. I knew I had to calm down, speak slowly and tell her what happened. She checked me over and said I had no broken bones or internal injuries and declared it was just bruising and soreness. She gave me an injection that really hurt and a prescription. I walked to the first chemist I saw and dropped off my prescription before crossing the street to the post office where I mailed Della's dog-pack back to Yasmin. Then I saw the camping store and bought a headlamp and a fly net for my hat. The injection had started to work so I decided, since I was in town, I should finish buying supplies so that I could stay at the Showground to relax and heal the following day. I picked up my script and went to the stores shopping for socks, underwear, and Blistex for my lips. While at Target I had a leg spasm, so I decided to hurry and get back but realised I had way too many bags to walk back to the showground. I approached a couple who were getting into their ute and asked for a lift. They were very nice and dropped me off at the Showground and I told them how grateful I was. Although I had some negative encounters with locals throughout my trip, there were far more generous people who, without them, I am sure this trip would have failed. I dropped off my bags with my supplies and limped over to talk to Nathan, the transporter driver. I asked if I could buy a bale of loose hay for the horses and he gave me one. Our long chat was interrupted by a call from the stock route government office. I talked to a lady about the map for about thirty minutes. She explained it all and told me that water points were 10 to 20 kilometers apart and that signs were posted. I had to put up my swag, so I left and set it up and returned to Nathan, and ate the potato salad I'd bought from Woolies, while Nathan checked out my maps. We had a great heart-to-heart. He read me a poem he'd written about his gorgeous pixie girlfriend and I thought that he was a very talented writer. The pills were starting to work, so I headed off to my swag. I woke in the middle of the night in pain and I took two more tablets. Lucky woke me up whinnying goodbye to the four horses that the transporter was taking away. I stayed in the swag until about 7:30am. I was just so terribly sore. I rose and fed the horses before putting up the tarp to give us shade later in the day. Whilst cleaning the animals medical supply bag, the nice couple that had given me a lift the day before, stopped by to check on me, saying they were worried about me. I thanked them for their kindness and assured them that I was doing well before washing Lucky's legs and removing the bindis. Della, Lucky and I headed for Roma to the vet, across the street from the Showground and Lucky whinnied goodbye to Chockie all the way. Will, the vet was very helpful, checking Della, pronouncing her fit. He looked at her wire scratched paw and gave her vaccinations, and I received a heap of medical supplies for future use. I began feeling very faint and had to sit down, and the receptionist brought me a glass of water. Feeling better, we went outside to look at Lucky's rear hooves. The vet said they were healing fine and gave Lucky his tetanus/strangles injection and worm paste. With a heavy heart, I paid the $364.70 bill, collected the supplies and left. We strolled back to the Showground and Chockie was there waiting at the gate for us. He doesn't seem to like to be separated from Lucky who was in the corral. I fed Della her new quality dog food from the vet. After a rest, I washed my clothes in a bucket, organised my supplies and took a nap. I woke to find Ben from The Western Star Newspaper had emailed me an invitation to dinner at the pub at 7pm. The day had heated up so I hosed down both horses with water. *We will have to get used to this weather… it's so hot to be in the sun.* I stayed in the shade almost all day. Traveling at night had become more realistic. I understood why my favourite adventurer Sharon, author of 'The Colour of Courage', preferred it. Della slept under the picnic table in the shade, and around 5pm, I put the horses into a grassier paddock offered by the caretaker. My shower finished just as Ben arrived to take me to the Irish pub for dinner. He was great company, and bought me a drink. We ordered salmon with mashed potatoes that I really enjoyed. Ben had worked as a rigger before he became a journalist, and wants to write for food magazines. He dropped me back at the Showground and I put on my boots and walked Lucky to the water trough, Chockie followed. After they both drank, I walked them back out to the grassy paddock, fed Della dinner and fell into bed exhausted.

Lucky, Della and Chockie

Chapter Three

Lucky

I climbed out of my swag around 7:30am and readied the horses for a trial ride on Lucky, adjusting the reins and the girth strap from the pack saddle. I led Lucky toward some people at a caravan camping site and asked the man to watch while I mounted, as this was Lucky's first time with someone on his back. Tying Lucky to a rail, I mounted him. He seemed surprised and moved sideways, but then stood still. I sat talking softly to him before dismounting and untying the reins, placing them over his neck. Once again I mounted him, made a clicking sound with my mouth and moved my heel into his side. He jumped sideways but then started walking. As I used the reins, I quickly realised he was used to being a harness racing horse. I didn't want to startle him and gave gentle 'turn left and right' instructions that he followed. We walked around for a while and I liked how Lucky performed - much smoother than Chockie but when I wanted him to stop, he didn't. I even tried saying 'stop'. When I pulled back on the reins he slowed down. I tried walking him up to a fence but he'd just turn and walk alongside the fence, so the only way to dismount was while he continued walking, which startled him. I placed the lead rope on Choco-chip and again mounted Lucky and rode him around with Choco-chip following. Everything went fine - Lucky even went into a trot for a while without me asking and gave me hope for the coming days. The day had begun to heat up so, after rinsing Lucky with cold water, I saddled Choco-chip, adjusted the cropper and loaded two bags. He didn't like it, but he followed me around. I think he wanted to be with Lucky, because he kept looking over at him. It seemed like a good omen that he liked Lucky's company. At 1am the next day, I rose and loaded the horses wearing my new headlamp, which worked a treat. At first, the light startled Chockie but he soon became used to it. Chockie was easy to pack because he was short and I didn't have to reach up as high. After a couple of hours, we were on the road. We travelled along the back roads of Roma and managed to pick up a little miniature black pony. It came out of nowhere and started following us. It slowed the horses down because they wanted to sniff and talk to it. The pony would stop in front of Lucky and then Lucky would stop too, so I had to dismount and shoo the pony away. This happened a few times after which I gave up and just walked the horses. The pony was not much bigger than Della, but it was fat and kept chasing Della away she would do a runner with her tail between her legs. We passed by a yard that had about four horses and the little black pony stopped to chat with them and didn't follow us. I wondered if it found its way home again, as it walked about six kilometers with us. The horses weren't interested in having a drink at the first creek we came to nor when we came across water troughs at Hodgson. Whilst Della drank, I was very worried as the next drink for the horses was ten kilometers away and it had begun to heat up. We continued on to Ross Creek where we had planned to spend the night. Lucky decided to do a bit of a run and I was holding onto Choco-chip's lead rope, I was pulled off balance, and fell off. My right knee and chest hurt. I managed to get up and back on Lucky grateful I hadn't been trampled. Falling off a horse hurts, but being stomped on by four hooves is much more painful.

The lady from the Stock Route government office had claimed all the water points noted on the map had water, but when we arrived at our next water point, Ross Creek was dry and empty. We had no choice but to continue on to Muckadilla, which was another ten kilometres. The horses had already walked 35 kilometres in the heat and I felt so sorry for them. But as they saying goes, "you can lead a horse to water, but you can't make it drink". The fly netting on my hat worked great. Occasionally one would get under, but they were easy to catch and kill. Suddenly, Lucky decided to do another runner, but this time I let go of Chockie's rope and held onto Lucky, pulling him back until he finally slowed down. It was 2pm when we arrived at Muckadilla a long walk without a drink. I gave the horses buckets of water at the rest stop before going to the hotel and booking 'Room 9' for the night. I put Lucky on the picket line and Chockie in hobbles as John, the hotel owner, brought a wheelbarrow full of water for the horses. After I filled up the green bucket with water for Della and gave her food near my hotel door she fell asleep straight away with a full tummy and a cozy bed. After a shower and rest I hosed Lucky but couldn't be bothered trying to catch Choco-chip. I placed Lucky on the picket line with a nosebag of grain, as there was little grass, and went into the hotel to chat with Sue and John, the owners of the hotel. They phoned a drover in Amby, arranging for me to have a chat with them when I arrived. By late afternoon I was starving, however I was not able to stomach much because of the intense pain I was in from my fall beforehand. I woke at 4am and we were on the road by daybreak. It was freezing but the stock route was lovely and off the highway. We saw our first live wild emus running around, about four, and big kangaroos, skinks, a tan snake (we took a large detour around it) and came to the first water spot where Della and Lucky had a good drink, but Chockie once again wasn't interested.

Chockie had spooked a few times and had run forward but Lucky stopped and Chockie had nowhere to go - Lucky seemed to have a calming effect on him. Finally, we arrived at the watering point in Amby. I unloaded the horses, placed Chockie in hobbles and Lucky on a picket line, and walked to the Amby store. The shop owner called the hospital in Mitchell to find if they had an X-ray machine as I was having problems breathing and it hurt more than yesterday. I felt as if my sternum may have been cracked so I needed to go to the hospital for X-rays. I had lunch, bought a copy of the newspaper, and read the article on us before returning to camp, putting Lucky in hobbles and dumping water on both horses. Della was sleeping in the shade, so I woke her and put her in the water trough. She liked it and stayed there for a while. The heat increased and Smokey, the drover showed up and put a rope noseband on the reins that will hopefully help Lucky stop pulling away so much. He explained that I need another set of reins for Lucky as mine were too small. He invited me over for a shower and dinner so I set up camp, fed Della, and grabbed some clothes. Smokey drove me to his son's place, and I had a shower and a drink. We had a good talk about his droving days and he gave me advice. He assured me that there is water in the Northern Territory. He had driven through the north of Australia, sometimes nine months at a time. He showed me where he lived, and the route to take tomorrow before he dropped me off at camp. I checked on the horses and went to bed.

I woke at 2am and packed before getting Lucky, he wouldn't move and he usually would be walking towards me in the morning because it's grain time. I did everything I knew but he wouldn't move. I noticed that he wasn't putting weight on his front left leg. I felt his leg it was hot between his body and knee although it didn't feel broken. Somehow he hurt his front left leg while on the picket line but I couldn't tell how it had happened. Distressed, I rushed to the drover's house for help. I knocked and woke him up, explaining the problem, but as it was 3am and Smokey said he would come by later in the morning. I walked back to camp, fed and watered Lucky and Chockie, hoping it's a good sign he's still interested in eating and drinking. Smokey showed up early, took one look and said it was Lucky's shoulder. I had to agree the shoulder appeared swollen and it looked like it had dropped. We went to Tony's house and I did some research on the Internet about horses' dislocated shoulders. It looked promising; it could be put back in place but would take time to heal. I called the Roma Vet and arranged to take Lucky to them. Smokey contacted a local family who lent a horse-float on which we loaded Lucky onto the float leaving Chockie behind in Amby in the yard of Smokey's house. We arrived at the Vet who took eight x-rays. He was having problems because the swelling was so big and the x-ray machine couldn't penetrate - he thought it looked like a fracture between the shoulder and elbow. He said if it's a dislocation then there was hope for a recovery but a fracture could not be helped. Terribly upset, I explained to the vet that to me, Lucky is not just a horse he is my baby. At four years old he had a long life ahead of him and I would help him. Lucky was as human to me as someone with a child. The only difference was that Lucky couldn't talk the conventional way. Lucky had learned to communicate with me in his own way. He would shove his nose in my back when he wanted me to wipe the flies from his face, stick his tongue out when he wanted water, put his head on my shoulder when he wanted a scratch behind the ears, he would come and sniff my back pocket when he wanted a carrot or two, and so much more. The vet suggested we take Lucky to Oakey Horse Hospital to get clearer X-rays as Oakey had more facilities than Roma and specialised in horses. So he booked an appointment at Oakey and arranged transport.

I went over everything that had happened, trying to discover how Lucky had harmed himself. It couldn't have been the picket line because it wasn't pulled tight at the base, and he had no damage on his skin. If Chockie had kicked him with his shod hooves it would have left a mark. The only thing I could think was that maybe he'd stepped in a hole and twisted his leg. I tied up Della in the shed next to the stables and gave her a bucket of water and food when my lift to Roma Hospital arrived. At the hospital I couldn't stop crying. I could see they thought I was crying in pain, but I was actually distraught about Lucky. A lovely nurse ran around and gave me lunch, took an EKG, tested my urine and assured me that I wasn't pregnant. Despite my misery, I had to laugh and I told her I actually knew that already. Finally, I saw the doctor, who ordered a pain injection, and chest X-ray. I waited for the X-ray technician to come back from lunch. After being given the injection and pain tablets, I ended up falling asleep on the bed to be woken by the X-ray lady. On the way my phone rang it was the vet with bad news, but he didn't want to tell me over the phone. I wanted to return to the vet clinic immediately, I had an anxious wait for the doctor to come back from his lunch break to tell me my results. The nurse comforted me while I cried and confided to her what had happened to Lucky and the doctor returned to explain I hadn't broken anything - probably torn the cartilage connecting my ribs to my sternum. He gave me a prescription which I filled it at the hospital and got a taxi to hurry me back to the vet. Arriving at the clinic, I checked on Lucky who was still in the same place, standing and eating. Will the vet told me he had sent Lucky's X-rays to the Oakey Horse Hospital where the horse specialist saw a broken bone between Lucky's shoulder and elbow. I replied I wanted to put a cast on it, or put pins in to connect his bones and help him through his rehabilitation but the vet's expression told me the answer. Shaking his head he told me it wasn't that easy with a horse. A feeling of dread came over me as I explained Lucky was my baby, not just a horse he was my best friend, my mate, my child, my responsibility. I would do everything I could to make him better. I didn't want to hear bad news. I knew that, in the past, horses were put down because of breaks but surely by now modern techniques and medicines were being used. Will showed me a chart of a horse skeleton and Lucky's X-rays. He pointed to the obvious break in Lucky's bone and even I could see it was in a hard place to fix. I hadn't realised the shoulder and elbow were part of a horse's main body. This was the news I had been dreading and I burst into tears as he suggested I spend time with Lucky. Della and I checked on Lucky in the stall and I watched him placing all his weight on his back legs while lifting the front of his body off the ground. He was trying to take weight off his good front leg, and I could see it was starting to swell due to the pressure being placed on it. Crying, I went to Lucky, putting my arms round his sore leg, lifting it off the ground, trying to take some of the weight for him. I frantically thought of ways to help him - *putting straps around his middle to hold the front of him off the ground - to help keep the weight off his sound front leg.*

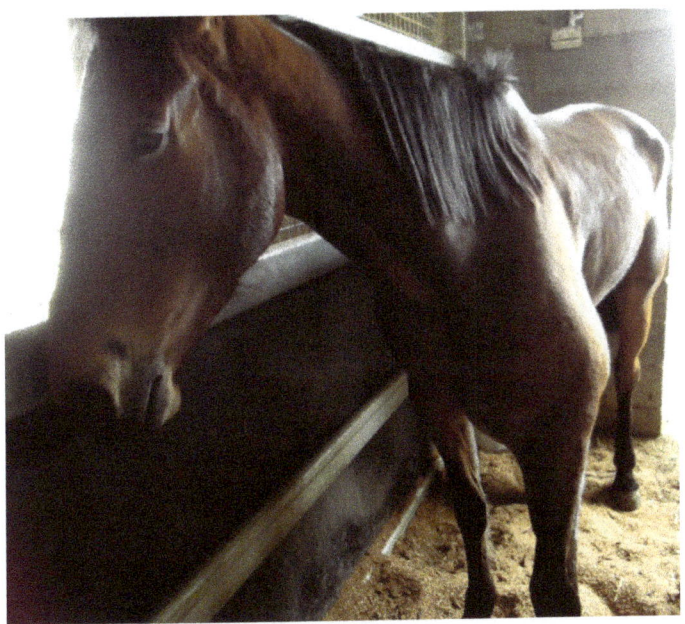

Lucky in the stable at the vet clinic with his broken shoulder

Lucky loved Della too, always rubbing his nose against Della's side and Della in return would lick Lucky's nose. Lucky was always full of love for both of us and we couldn't let him down in his hour of need. We sat there thinking we could both be with him and do our best to help Lucky back to health. Grief-stricken, I could only weep as I scratched behind his ears, wiped the flies from his eyes and put my arms around his neck, hugging him. Lucky had been the best horse, with me 24/7 and we had bonded. He'd always walked to me when I wanted him and sometimes even when I didn't want him too. Carrying our gear, he'd followed Della and I across Australia and had even carried me for the last two days. He had been the friendliest horse and had done so much for us. Without Lucky, there would have been no walk, because Della and I couldn't have carried our supplies on our own. Will came and quietly explained he couldn't put on a cast. In reality, I had known this after he'd shown me the horse anatomy pictures; all he could do was give Lucky a painkiller. The swelling had stopped growing, but the broken leg was now three times the size of Lucky's sound leg. As the good front leg kept swelling, Lucky again started lifting his front legs off the ground, backed into the brick wall of the stable, rubbing his hind-end on the brick. The hair on his tail started disintegrating and this upset me. I knew he was hurting himself whilst trying to get rid of his terrible pain. I asked Will to give him more pain killers but he replied that, more injections would make him relax and he would fall down and injure himself. By this time I was beside myself. I couldn't take Lucky's pain away, I could feel it but couldn't make him better. I would have done anything to swap places with him. I knew I could live with an amputated leg but realised Lucky couldn't. Already his good front leg was swelling from the extra weight on it. I had to accept his broken bone couldn't be put in a cast; it couldn't be pinned or screwed back together. Horses can't lie down for long periods of time as this causes internal damage so Lucky couldn't even have 'bed rest'. Now Lucky was injuring himself and I begged him to stop backing into the brick wall. I brought his bucket of water to distract him and he took a long drink, than went back to lifting his front legs off the ground and backing into the wall. By this time his tail was hairless with bone showing

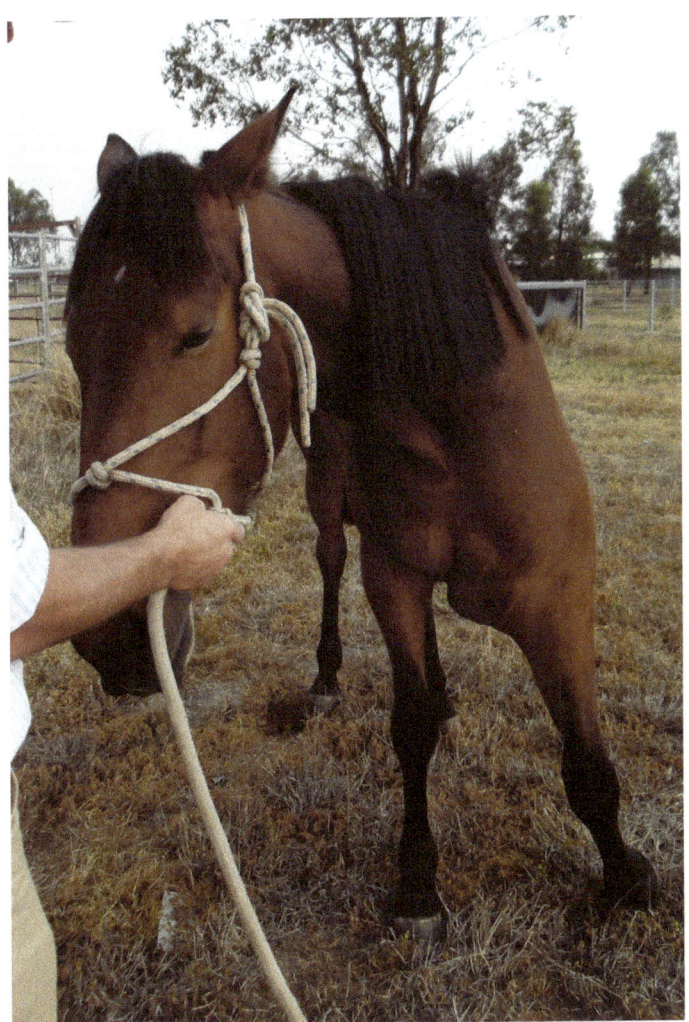

Lucky in terrible pain- The worst day of my life

and I was frantic with worry. Lucky's broken leg just hung low and we couldn't help him with his pain. I knew he couldn't be left in this state. Lucky would have to be put down. I confided in Will that I just didn't know what else to do. Will sat me down and explained the procedure. We would walk Lucky around the back of the stables, and he would give Lucky an injection in his neck that would put him 'under,' as if he were going into surgery. After this he would be given an overdose and Lucky wouldn't wake up, he would fall to the ground rather quickly but he would no longer be in pain.

Della and I had our photo taken with Lucky before we walked him around to the back of the stables. It took some time as Lucky had to hop along on his front leg and mostly used his rear legs. I petted Lucky's face whilst Will emptied the syringe into Lucky's neck then pulled out another one and gave him the second injection. Overcome with grief, I stepped back as Lucky started falling. He fell on his side and I quickly bent over him patting his neck, keeping the flies from his eyes and burying my face in his mane and neck. Whilst Will used his stethoscope to see if Lucky was breathing, I sobbed, feeling completely wretched. Suddenly I felt drops of water on the back of my head and realised it was the sky crying for Lucky. After months of drought, the sky dropped tears of sympathy for him. Will wanted to show me that I had done the right thing by Lucky. We turned Lucky over and he had me feel the break in his leg. I stayed with Lucky till the sun set, petting him, brushing the straw out of his hair, mostly just crying and hugging him. I cut a piece of Lucky's mane to keep and Della curled up against his backbone it would've been the first time Della lay so close to Lucky for a long period. I knew I was going to miss feeding Lucky carrots, having him prod me in the back with his nose, follow me around the campsite, poking his nose in my swag as we walked across Australia. Lucky had been my best friend. I always thought it would be the three of us, Lucky, Della and I looking over the Indian Ocean at the end of our trip, I had never even considered the possibility that one of us wouldn't make it. If anything, I figured I would be the first one to die. In fact, I couldn't have imagined Della or Lucky would die before me because I knew that I would do everything possible to keep them alive and now here I was, alive, and Lucky dead and we'd only been on the road for a month. Repeatedly I asked myself how I could have prevented this accident from happening. Not knowing what had caused the break, I wondered if I had picked Lucky a grassier, softer, level area, it could have been prevented. Soon it was dark and I couldn't see. I went into the shed and lay on the saddle blankets with Della next to me. The sky cried all night too.

I woke up early to see the bloke taking Lucky away had arrived. I unlocked the gate and he drove a front-end loader with a bucket attached at the front. He scooped Lucky up and then drove to a tipper truck, raised the bucket and dropped Lucky inside the back of the truck. Again I sobbed my heart out when Damian arrived with the horse float and Choco-chip and I put Chockie in a paddock behind the vet clinic. After filling his water and giving him a nose bag full of grain, I went inside with a heavy heart. I paid the vet bill for Lucky - it cost almost seven hundred dollars. Although I would have paid more than double that if had meant Lucky could have received treatment and survived. I left the vet clinic and John Riley pulled up in a little red car. He jumped out and gave me a hug and then I had him drive around back to pick up my gear and Della. I was glad he had come, because I didn't want to spend the whole day alone, thinking about Lucky and what a horrible person I was. John was really kind and talked to me for the four hour drive to Augbigny whilst I held Tara, his little dog on my lap and Della slept in the back not too happy about another dog so close to me. After lunch we drove to Toowoomba, while John had a few errands, I went to the Post Office to buy envelopes and stamps to send letters. We came back to Augbigny and found Morris had stopped by for a visit whilst we were out so I texted him. Later, he came for a drink and we arranged for him to collect Della and I at 7am to drive to Roma to pick up Choco-chip. I went to bed shortly after as I hadn't slept much the night before.

Morris arrived with the horse float and Della sat in the back seat of his ute. Morris was very friendly and answered the many questions that I had. It kept my mind from thinking of Lucky. Della became car sick and I felt bad as she'd soiled Morris's towel and sleeping bag. I put Della on my lap and she was fine for the rest of the journey. We took a different scenic route to Roma where we stopped off at the Roma vet and picked up the rest of my gear and Choco-chip. While I shared email addresses with the vet, Morris had to run around the paddock to catch Chockie. I'd forgotten to tell Morris that I had trained Chockie by holding up the nose bag and rewarding Chockie with grain, when he walked over to me. With Chockie loaded, we were on the road again. We stopped at Queensland's oldest Roma winery, sampling a few wines and Morris liked the Mist bottle, a sweet style of white wine so I bought him a bottle. I ordered takeaway and ate it at a rest stop while Morris had a beer and I had a glass of wine with our lunch as Della ran around. I think she remembered that we had visited this rest stop a week ago. We headed for Surat which has a lovely river and the Cobb Co. Museum before heading for Glenmorgan where we stopped at the pub and had a drink and chat with the locals. We stopped off at Morris' house and dropped off Choco-chip then he drove Della and I back to John's. I warmed up by the fire before having an early night, still exhausted from the previous day's emotions, and a long day in the ute.

I slept late the next day, before cleaning the kitchen after breakfast. Heidi and I spent some time on the Internet looking for a horse. I found a standard-bred called 'Night' up for adoption in Beaudesert I phoned and talked to Wayne, the owner, who he said he would call me back if it was okay for me to come and have a look tomorrow. Morris arrived to drop off my gear and agreed to look at 'Night' tomorrow if I was able to go. Later, John and I had dinner at the Aubigny Hotel and ran into Morris. Wayne had called to say that someone else was coming to look at his horse so I checked the Internet and found another horse, a pretty painted gelding and Morris agreed to have a look in the morning. Sunday morning arrived and Morris showed up at 7am. John had advised us to arrive early to see how hard the horse would be to catch. When we arrived, the cutest boy answered the door. I checked him over and informed him that his trouser fly was down. He fixed it and we drove around back to look at the gelding. At first glance, I was pretty sure that Morris wouldn't approve of the horse because of how skinny it was and the unusual dent in his hip. We were told that he had been injured when he was six months old and the vet had removed a piece of hipbone that had broken off.

Chapter Four

Charlie the Brumby

On the way back to John's, I mentioned to Morris that I was interested in another horse and Morris pulled his blue ute over and we called and talked to the owner, David Berman. He agreed to us coming to take a look at Charlie the brumby – it turned out we were only five minutes' drive away and David was still in his pyjamas when we arrived. We walked out back with him and he had quite a few horses, mostly show-jumpers. My first impression of Charlie was 'a fat pony'. So I thought lazy. However, Morris's first impression was excitement. He thought this pony was just what I needed although he joked about sending Charlie to visit 'Jenny Craig'. Charlie was a little hard to catch and Morris had first go in the saddle. Morris liked him and said that Charlie could 'cover ground'. Apparently, David's daughter had used Charlie for show jumping competitions, and he'd rescued Charlie from the Greenbank Military Base when he was six months. Now eight, Charlie stood 14.3 hands. Morris was enthusiastic, so I gave Charlie a go in the saddle but kept him away from the jumping area. I wasn't ready to go hurtling over wooden poles yet. Della didn't take much notice of Charlie and Charlie just gave her a wary stare.

Morris watched me in dismay and declared I needed to be taught how to properly mount and dismount safely from a horse. I had just been grabbing the saddle horn with both hands and pulling myself up. Then I swung my leg over and slide down when dismounting but Morris started talking about Risk Assessment and Safety around horses. I think he teaches workplace health and safety at the riding pens. After Morris had a proper feel around Charlie's legs and hooves and a long chat with David. I agreed to buy Charlie. David's wife arrived and said Charlie would normally sell for $1,800.00 but since he was going to a good home, I could get him for $1,000.00. She gave me her business card so I could email her and receive the banking details. When we left, Morris suggested I really needed to be taught to ride correctly and offered to do it. I packed some camping gear, swag, food, and of course Della and I left a note to John that I'd be gone for a few days. We drove to Morris' place and collected his camping gear and loaded up his three year-old gelding Ironstein before heading to the feedlot where he worked. I borrowed Brannum to practice my riding skills. Stopping only at a grocery store to pick up a few things (Morris even bought dog food for Della) we headed for the hills with me looking forward to this teaching trip. After driving down a dirt road, we arrived at Pat's property. She came and unlocked the gate and I sat in the back with Della so Pat could sit up front. We drove down her long driveway and arrived at her stable. Pat, who lives in a caravan on her property and rents her house, is a very lovely lady and I liked her from the start. She had many horses wandering around and seven dogs - she preferred tiny ones. Della was the biggest dog there and Della isn't big at all. She also had two birds that talked and a baby

Joey she'd rescued. I could tell from the start that Pat and I were going to get along very well.

We unloaded Morris' horses and saddled them to go for a ride. We walked down the dirt road with me listening to Morris delivering his instructions. It was a lovely country and I was eager to learn. By the time we returned and unsaddled, it was tea time. The campfire was built underneath an upside down shopping trolley. It was most interesting and very useful. The Billy could be kept on the lower shelf (child seat) or directly in the fire. The washing up pot was kept on the top shelf. In addition, there were two levels of heating, the bottom or upper shelf. *Who knew shopping trolleys could be used for more than carting your stuff around?* Morris cleaned out the back of his horse float, put his swag in there to sleep,

Riding with Pat in Maryvale

and then, since it was now dark, turned his headlights on for me to set up my swag. I set up in a small yard in front of the ute, closing the gate to keep the curious horses out. I had forgotten to pack my thermals, a mistake as it became very cold up there. Next morning, after toast and a hot drink we took off for another educational ridding lesson.

Morris's Instructions on Horses:

1) After unloading the horse float, tie the horses up for a while, to let them think about it.
2) If the horse doesn't do what you want, tie the horse up for a while, leave the horse alone, to let the horse think about it.
3) Always mount a horse standing next to the shoulder, with your bum facing his nose, stirrup turned, and elbow in the side of neck. Mount with one hand on saddle and the other hand holding the reins.
4) Dismounting a horse is a smooth fluid motion, swing the leg over and land on the ground facing the rear end of the horse, near the shoulder. The horse always appreciates a good view of your bum.
5) Never walk up to a horse front on, always approach on the side.
6) Place your hand between the hoses ears when putting on a halter or reins.
7) Never force the bit into the mouth, play with his mouth for a little.
8) When removing the reins always let the horse drop the bit, never pull the bit out.
9) When placing the saddle blanket on a horse always put it in the correct place and position and don't drop it. Gently place the blanket on.

10) When placing the saddle gently on, don't let the stirrups and girth swing down and hit the horse on the side. Walk over to the other side and put them in the correct position.
11) While saddling the horse, leave the reins dangling over the side of your arm.
12) While riding the horse, keep your back straight or Morris will put a broomstick thru your elbows. Keep your knees close to the side of the horse or you will have to hold a cigarette paper with your knees against the side of the horse. Heels down, heels down, heels down.
13) While holding the reins, keep them low over the horses' neck. The rein comes up thru the bottom of your hand and then between your thumb and index finger.
14) While turning a horse, your opposite foot presses into the horse and your other foot comes away from the horse.
15) Always do a Risk Assessment when approaching an unknown horse.
16) Don't let an unknown horse approach another horse to say Hello.
17) When loading your horse onto the float, don't pull on the lead rope, let the horse think about it and then it will walk onto the float.
18) Never have scissors around a horse. It is a cardinal sin to cut a horse's tail/mane.
19) Stroke the neck and pat the ass.

For a while, we rode down a lovely path in the mountains, but it petered out and we had to ride through thick bush. Thankfully, my drover jacket and hat protected my arms and head against the tree branches as we pushed through but my knees were sore from banging against tree trunks and climbing up and down some very steep hills. When we arrived at a hill that looked vertical, I refused. I could just see my horse falling head first down that steep incline and me flying off too. So instead, we headed back and cooked breakfast, which to me was a much better idea. One of Pat's injured horses needed attention so Morris and I headed into town to get mobile reception and call Monica, the vet. She met us straight away and followed us to the horse. Pat walked Boogy, the ten year-old black gelding, who was limping and trying not to use his rear leg. He had a severe deep cut, which Monica cleaned. After applying gauze and wrapping it well, she used duct tape to hold it in place and gave Boogy a few injections, before inserting a microchip. Morris and I found a gate for a horsebox in the stable and we walked Boogy into the box for the night. The bore pump didn't work, so Pat filled up a bucket of water for Boogy and I fed him some Lucerne hay.

Later, Morris took me for another ride in the hills, but this time we kept to the paddocks and paths, with me receiving Morris's non-stop instructions throughout the ride. I was just glad I stayed in the saddle; it's a good day when I don't fall off. That's all I was aiming for, just to stay in the saddle. The last fall hurt and my chest was still sore, especially when I did a movement that used that area. Mounting a horse hurt like hell as Morris wouldn't let me use two hands, and leg muscles and biceps to pull myself up. Mounting one handed I had to use one bicep, my leg muscles and chest muscles and that was too painful so Morris helped me by giving my bum a lift. Since Morris won't be with me on the walk, I had yet to figure another way to get my bum in that saddle without using my chest muscles. Later that evening I made toast and baked beans for dinner and Pat talked about her life, which I found fascinating. That night I slept much better as Morris gave me his extra blanket to use.

In the morning we helped Pat build a yard for Boogy, stringing new wire through the posts and stacking tires along the sides that we tied up. The yard looked really good and I my heart went out to Boogy. I hoped he healed quickly and fed him some oaten hay and then cooked breakfast before Morris offered. Morris had left eggshell in yesterday's breakfast and I didn't want to pick eggshell out again. Maybe he did that on purpose to ensure I'd cook. After breakfast, I folded the swag and we loaded the ute with the horses and gear and headed off. I arrived back at John's in the afternoon and took a long bubble bath. The bath water was the color of a cow dam, the result of not showering for three days and camping in the dirt. I scrubbed my fingers and tried hard to dislodge the dirt from under my nails. When I dried off and looked for my clothes, I found I had only one pair of clean jeans. All my shirts were in the washing machine so I borrowed one of John's shirts and wore that. I checked my emails and David Berman had contacted me about another brumby that one of his mates had for sale so I called Morris who collected me and we went to inspect. The Brumby was a five year-old gelding but very tall, too tall for me to use as a pack horse. Morris and I both rode him but I didn't feel confident riding. This horse was taller than Lucky and I was frightened that I wouldn't ever stand up if I fell off this one. We thanked the guy and left. Morris dropped me at John's house and after dinner and later I found an email from David confirming receipt of the bank transfer, inviting me to collect Charlie. So I called Morris and he agreed we could collect Charlie the following day. This was the first positive news since Lucky's death.

I found Charlie easy to lead mainly because he didn't pull on the rope. After he had a think about it, he happily walked onto the float (Morris's rule Number 17). I had forgotten to bring any ropes but David gave me a role-halter and lead-rope as well as two bales of hay.

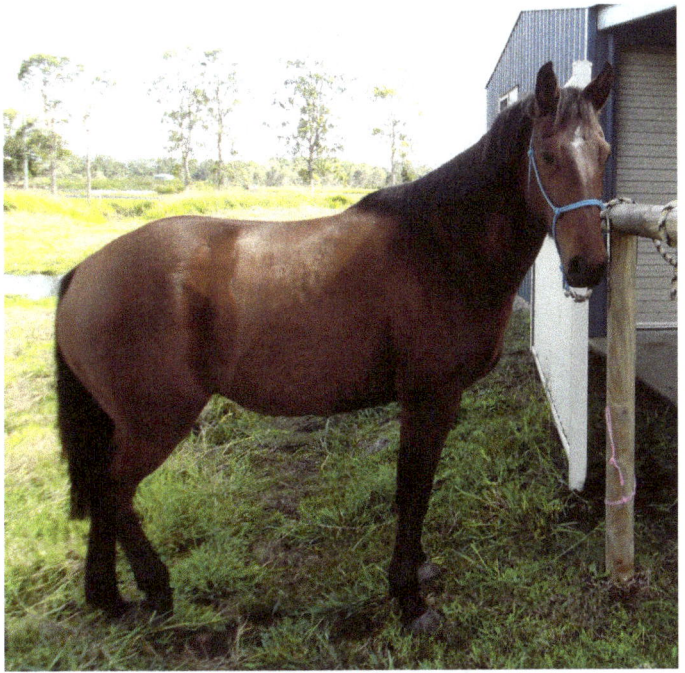

Charlie all cleaned up

Whilst Morris shod his horse Ironstein, I hosed the dirt off and, using a sheep shearer's comb, brushed the tangled mess that was Charlie's mane. Morris showed me how to lunge properly and I started lunging Charlie much to Della's excitement. She came into the yard barking and running around and I had to tell her to leave as she was distracting Charlie. Without Della, Charlie soon got the hang of it and Morris took us back to John's. In the morning, I rose early and mopped and vacuumed the floor, changed the bed sheets, and did the laundry and dishes before Della and I started to walk to Morris' place to work with Charlie. It was hot and it felt like I had walked more than the eight kilometers so ended up hitching and a nice lady picked us up and dropped us off at Morris' place. First thing I did was to check Charlie and I was pleased he was doing fine in the round yard. I opened the stables and went straight to work doing some lunging with him. Charlie was doing so well I tried lunging without the rope. He moved into a walk but then didn't stop so I reattached the lead-rope. He drank water from the green collapsible bucket with no problems, I brushed his mane some more and gave it a bit of a trim but had to attach hobbles on his front legs and tied him up as he wouldn't let me near his tail. Then Charlie pulled back and broke his halter. He kept moving around to the side, so I couldn't touch his tail and I ended up putting David's halter back on him. Later in the afternoon, I dumped a bucket of water on him to cool him off and gave him a break in a tiny fenced yard that had some grass and weeds growing. Charlie had an afternoon snack before some more lunging, which he was responding to very well. I cleaned his front hooves with the hoof-pick, but Charlie wouldn't let me near his back feet. When Morris returned from work, I showed him Charlie's lunging and he drove me back to John's. The next morning, before dropping me at Morris', I loaded up the back of John's car with all my gear and helped him service his mare with his stud, a huge Welsh Cobb horse that acted crazy and was all over the place. I checked on Charlie who seemed keen to see me, walking towards me when I approached. I started with a bit of lunging then tried to put a blanket on him but he wouldn't allow me. So I put the hobbles on and succeeded with the blanket, followed by the pack-saddle. I lunged him around with him carrying the saddle and he didn't seem to mind the middle strap. I tried lunging him without the lead-rope and he responded quite well. It took him a few steps to stand still when I said 'Whoa' but Charlie was improving. I cleaned his front hooves again and tried the back hooves again, but that was still a 'no go' area so I hosed him down with water to cool him off. I walked him back to the round yard and tied him up so he wouldn't roll in the dirt but somehow Charlie still managed to roll on one side. I swear that brumby loved to be covered in dirt. I brushed the dirt off and brushed out his mane, having to constantly tell him to stand still, but he just kept moving around.

When John arrived, he wasn't impressed with Charlie and also reminded me that I have to move out as he is expecting visitors. I needed to find somewhere else to stay, which depressed me, as I still felt sad after losing Lucky. I had been checking the Internet and found what I hoped was the perfect horse in Stanthorpe which was two and-a-half hours' drive away. I hoped Morris approved. Morris arrived after work at sunset at his place. I had filled my solar powered shower for him in the morning but the water had cooled. However, Morris took a shower and said he liked it. We climbed into his ute and Della was immediately sick, the second time she has spewed in his ute, we hadn't even pulled out of the driveway. Morris was pretty good, as most people would have complained. I had Della sit on the floor, with her head by my lap so I would know if she was going to be ill but Della made it back without any more accidents. Back at John's I cooked dinner and he offered me use of his car to look at the pony in Stanthorpe. I called the seller and arranged for the next day. I was so happy the pony was still available as so many of the ones I found had already been sold. I talked to Heidi and we agreed that I would stop by her place in the morning to see if she would like to go with me to Stanthorpe to look at a pony.

Later that evening, Morris called and informed me that the lady who lives in the house where he rents the stables complained I'm overworking Charlie in the heat. I insisted I wasn't and explained what we did the whole day. I had dumped water or hosed him down during the hottest part of the day, also tying him in the shade under the tree for a while. Morris had wanted me to work Charlie hard, but I couldn't go for very long, because it made me dizzy turning in circles while lunging. I had spent most of the day brushing him, cleaning his hooves, and petting him, so that he knew me. After the phone call I was quite upset, but John sympathised and told me not to worry about people who have no lives and liked to make up stories. The next morning, I drove John's car, collecting Heidi and arrived at Stanthorpe to find the pony was small. The lady rode him around the round yard first but he just wasn't keen and wasn't listening to her. I mounted the pony and he trotted with a weird gait. I felt confident riding the pony, but he just didn't want to do anything I asked. Heidi asked the lady to take him for a canter, and Heidi showed me the pony was lame in the rear leg, the reason it was trotting weird. His leg buckled every other stride, which was my decision maker. Unfortunately, the pony wouldn't be able to handle the walking ahead of us. Thanking the lady, I told her the pony wasn't for me and we left. Back at John's, I loaded Della and went to visit Charlie and found Morris was already home. I lunged Charlie, giving him water and hay and filled my solar camp shower with water for Morris to use before heading back to John's as the sky was dark. On the Internet that night Heidi found another horse and said she would drive me to North Maclean if I could get a ride to her house. I called Di, who was selling the horse, and it sounded like the perfect horse for me. I told her I would call in the morning to confirm if I was coming out.

In the morning I explained things to John and he agreed to let me use his car so I called Heidi and Di and told them all 'I'm on my way'. I arrived at Heidi's and we attached the float to the back of the ute and loaded Della in the back of the ute knowing Della would be able to smell everything and love it. We arrived and I looked at Choco, knowing I would have to change his name because it would confuse everyone - I'd call him Jonesy, since my mate wanted a horse named after him. Choco was bigger than I thought he'd be but he seemed fine as he was saddled and taken to the yard. The trainer rode him around and then brought in a young horse they were breaking-in and showed how Choco could lead. I was interested as he had two lead ropes off the horse being led, the first one went around his horse's chest and the second one went directly to him. The end of the first rope was draped over the saddle and he held the end of the second rope in his hands. When the young horse stopped or spooked Choco pulled the young horse in line and seemed not to worry about the rope around his neck but I wondered whether Choco could handle Charlie as he was pretty big.

I received a helmet from one of the kids and mounted Choco. He had a slow walk, than went into a trot. I wanted a horse with a fast walk, *maybe he could improve*. With the cantering, I felt I was being thrown off his back. It could have been the round yard as I usually canter when the path is straight not in a tight circle. I felt confident in Choco it did not feel like he was about to take off any minute, quite the opposite, I was hard pressed to get him into a canter. His slow walk needed to improve into a fast walk and wondered if it could be taught. I checked his legs and hooves and impressed with the leading of the other horse, I decided to buy him.

Heidi and I began to notice the horses in the paddocks looked underfed and malnourished. Di said she'd only had Jonesy for six weeks, so he hadn't lost too much weight. I knew Morris wouldn't be too happy with the shape this new horse was in but I was sure it was nothing a better diet couldn't improve. The trainer and I went for a ride around the property and I talked money with Di. She was completely different to David who cared about Charlie and looked after his horses. David's horses were in fine shape, glossy coats and had good feed. David wanted Charlie to go to a loving home while Di was a horse dealer and she started going on about costs of feeding, worming, training, etc. It sounded like all the horses were a burden to her and she wanted them gone and didn't care who bought them as long as she made a profit. As a person with many animals in her care, I was very disappointed and thought she should be in another line of work. I had never tallied up the cost of quality Lucerne, hay, grain, carrots, and apples that Lucky had consumed. He had been my baby and whatever it cost, that's what I spent. After talking to Di and adjusting to the shock of someone talking about the horses' cost, we agreed on $2,200 having knocked $100 off her price. As Heidi knew, because I had looked at my bank account in the car as we were driving, I only had $2000 so Heidi loaned me the missing $200. I used Di's computer to transfer the money and we loaded up Jonesy. After dealing with these horse dealers, I appreciated Morris, Pat, and Heidi's way a lot more. I had always assumed that anyone who owned a horse would love it. People who don't love animals shouldn't have animals in their care and mistreating animals upsets me, not loving animals is mistreating them. Why would anyone want to own a living creature that's not loved or cared for properly?

Chapter Five

Jonesy

Jonesy unloaded reasonable well but he wanted to stop and have a 'sticky beak'. I walked him to the stall so he could be sprayed with tick repellant. After, Heidi loaded Jonesy in the float, while I went inside the office to fill out the paperwork and pay the fee. Jonesy had been quiet in the float and he travelled well. He didn't look upset when we stopped, but I opened the door to give him a carrot to munch on and I could tell he hadn't had a carrot for weeks. We dropped Jonesy off at Heidi's place as she couldn't drive to Oakey. Her daughter walked Jonesy into the round yard, Heidi fed him a biscuit of hay, and I left. I stopped off at Lorelle's as she was loaning me a saddle for the trip. I really appreciated it and hoped I would soon be able to buy my own and return hers. I felt bad having to borrow things from people but so grateful that they cared enough to offer. I stopped to put petrol in John's car and when I was pulling out onto the road, I saw lightening, a large flash in the sky and began to worry that Jonesy might be uncomfortable in a new place with a big storm on the horizon. Back at John's, I showed him pictures of the new horse, and after cooking dinner, phoned Morris. He suggested Jonesy be dropped off at John's place so he could come after work to check him over. He'd ride Jonsey to his place whilst I followed, driving his ute. I agreed and asked after Charlie as I hadn't seen him all day, but Morris said he'd fed him and let him wander round the yard. John had already told me that I would have to move on, so the next day, when I drove Morris' ute, I intended to place all my stuff in the back. I hadn't yet asked Morris if I could stay with him. Worried, I stressed in case he didn't agree and I'd have to find somewhere else to camp. John dropped me at Morris' and Charlie had his head over the gate, seeming happy to see me. I put the halter on and hobbled him that made it easier for me to brush him. Now more relaxed, Charlie allowed me groom his hindquarters - but not his tail. He tossed his head when I brushed his mane and I kept saying 'Stand', which was effective for a while but he soon forgot and moved again.

After dropping off Jonesy at John's, Heidi arrived at Morris' barn with a pair of her daughter's old riding boots. Whilst thanking her for the boots and her help with Jonesy, she expressed her concern that he'd been left in a small yard with no water or feed so, putting a biscuit in a bag and Della in the float, we headed back to John's place. In the heat of the day, I found a bucket and filled it with water for Jonesy before giving him the hay biscuit and he started eating whilst I brushed him and cleaned his hooves. Morris arrived right on time and I quickly asked if I could stay at his place. To my relief, he agreed. Morris looked Jonesy over and nodded, saying he looked fine. He saddled him up and off he rode. I packed my things into his ute and drove down the road after him, yelling from the window, 'How are you going?' He replied all was well and to meet him at the pub.

I pulled into the pub's parking lot and Morris expressed his concern. Jonesy had a tendency to spook at things, however Jonesy's spooking was much more sharp and sudden then Chockie's. I'd always had plenty of warning with Chockie, I could tell by his head movements. He would be eyeing the object and deciding if he should shy away before deciding 'this thing is scary' and only then he would spook. I had even tried covering Chockie's eye with my hand while he was looking at the 'scary' object in the past and at times, this worked. Morris asked me to go into the pub, buy his beer and meet him at his place. On the way out I encountered a man who told me in a very stern and threatening way that I wasn't welcome at his mother-in- law's home, the same lady who complained about me where Morris rented the stables. I received a real tongue-lashing. Morris had told me that he had asked if I could come over during the day to work with Charlie. This woman hadn't ever spoken to me. I left the pub upset and passed Morris, who called me over to let me know that the women had given him the same message. Morris explained that to keep the peace it was best if I did not come around to his place. I was no longer welcome. I took Jonesy's reins and walked down the street with Della. Morris said he would pick up his float and Charlie and drop me off at the Oakey Showground. He insisted I not ride Jonesy, as he needed more training. I started walking towards Oakey wearing Brea's boots, made for riding not walking, and my feet blistered in the first kilometer. The boots were a little big and my feet kept slipping around. I walked for quite a while, depressed and crying. Della ran ahead and then ran back, jumping up in the air; she looked definitely well rested and ready to go. Morris drove up in his ute with Charlie on board the float and he loaded Jonesy with no problems. I hopped in the back seat with Della and Morris drove us to the

Showground. When we arrived the front gate was locked so Morris drove down the side of the grounds on the dirt road and found an unlocked gate. It was dark at this stage and we couldn't see anything and had no idea where to put the horses, set up camp, or if we were even in the right area. We used the headlights to look for a paddock, but couldn't find one fully enclosed. The holding pens had large deep holes because they were being reconstructed so we decided the stables would have to do. We unloaded the horses and found some long wooden bars to use as gates to keep the horses in their separate stalls. I had to put Charlie in hobbles as we couldn't fix the side of his stall. Morris unloaded my stuff and left to drive back to his place to pick up the rest of my gear. In a dejected state, I filled up the water trough, watered, and fed the three of them.

Heidi phoned and asked me how I was and I explained situation. I was at the Oakey Showground, had arrived in the dark and hadn't asked permission from anyone. (We had looked for the caretakers' house but couldn't see it). So wonderful, caring Heidi told me not to worry and that she would sort it out and thankfully, she did! The caretaker, Amelia, phoned and told me she would come out to meet me. When she arrived, she was very nice, told me I was in the correct part of the Showground, and unlocked the bathrooms for me. A man named Joe, who worked with Morris at the feedlot, was staying at the Showground in a caravan and he came and had a drink with us. We needed a drink after the all the problems. Morris' landlady had informed him that 'strange women' were not allowed at the stables. I teased him that he was back, living at home with his parents. After Morris drank his six-pack of beer, he knew he couldn't drive home, so he helped me finish my wine, then pulled his swag out of his ute and set it up next to mine. Della slept on her blanket and we each climbed into our own swags. I checked on Charlie throughout the night. We had left Charlie in hobbles and Heidi had me troubled about having hobbles on horses. Another potential problem to worry about. Morris left early for work and I rose too. With Morris' saddle blanket underneath, I put the packsaddle on Charlie. Morris had forgotten to bring my saddle blankets but I thought things would be fine without the proper saddle blanket. I was wrong. At the beginning, everything went smoothly. Charlie became quite excited when he saw the racehorses running round the track so I placed one pack on each of his sides and led him round the Showground. I was in a large open area and opted to do some lunging with him wearing the packs. Charlie behaved well at first but after trotting it all went wrong. Without the special blanket, the packs bounced and whacked his sides when they came down. This startled him and he bucked. He continued to buck until the bag buckles snapped and flew off - which also startled him. Finally, Charlie galloped off to the stables, sighing; I picked up the bags and followed him back.

In the meantime, a jockey had yelled at me that Della was running around on the racetrack with the horses. Della just wanted to have fun, but I understood those racehorses would have been spooked with a strange dog running between their legs and the thought of Della being trampled on by a racehorse was frightening. So back at the stables I put Della on the leash not wanting to worry about her when I had the horses to focus on. Charlie was eating the grass outside his stall so I led him back inside and put up the wooden bars but left the packsaddle on so he could get used to it. Note to oneself: always tighten the saddle after a horse bucks because it will loosen up.

I came back moments later to find Charlie panting and the saddle and blanket on the ground. Walking to the saddle, I could see marks on the ground, so I think he just rolled until it came off. I took Charlie back to the stables and left him to calm down. I placed the blanket on Jonesy and then the packsaddle with no problems and led him back to the stables. Suddenly Jonesy started bucking. The lead rope went flying and Jonesy took off bucking across the showground. Feeling defeated, I walked back to the stables to get my leather gloves because the leadrope was dragging and I knew it would be covered in bindis. Joe's caravan door was open so I asked that if he saw Jonesy wandering, to please tie him up. Joe looked worried and stated the Showground wasn't fully enclosed it threw me into a panic. The way Jonesy had taken off he could be in Dalby in no time! I jumped into Joe's ute beside him, and we hastily drove around the roads that enclosed the Showground. Relieved, we found Jonesy with the packsaddle still on. He had stopped to eat grass with another horse but as we drove up Jonesy started bucking again and the horse with him also started to buck. Jonesy stopped as Joe walked to him so I took the lead rope and Joe unbuckled the offending packsaddle and put it and the blanket in the back of his ute. I walked Jonesy back to the yard to calm down and bond with Charlie. Back at Joe's caravan, we had a chat about what had happened. Joe explained the packsaddle and the strap had slipped too far back and that was causing the horse to buck. What would have happened had I been in the saddle? I would've landed in the next State! I decided to get Jonesy shod so Morris could take him to the feedlot (horses at the feedlot were required to be shod) and give him a few eight hour working days. I didn't want to get on Jonesy if he had that much energy. I have lost confidence in him after watching that latest display. I let the horses bond for a while, while I cleaned out their stalls with the wheelbarrow and shovel I borrowed from the workers at the Showground, and fixed the broken pack bags. Then I went to collect the horses. As I walked past the workers towards the horses I said 'Round Two!' They thought it was a great joke, all this free entertainment by Della and the horses. Jonesy arrived at the gate first so I put the lead-rope on him and walked him over to the water trough, and then placed him into his stall. Meanwhile Charlie was whinnying as if he missed his best friend. Charlie was waiting with his head over the gate when I returned to the paddock. After grooming the horses, I returned Jonesy and Charlie to the yard with a feeling that Jonesy would be the boss in their horsey relationship.

Jonesy and Charlie

Heidi emailed me that she intended to give Morris a talking-to about hobbles on horses and Lorelle wanted to give Morris a lecture on the spurs he wears. Poor Morris, he called to say he would stop by in the morning before work and drop off the saddle blankets and some more of my gear. As agreed, he arrived and said he would get me the worm paste for the horses and he came by after work again. I made the horses' rope halters out of pretty blue rope whilst they stood still. Jonesy went first; he was very patient while I wrapped the rope around his face and tried to figure it out. I had plenty of carrots for distraction when he became impatient. Then I started on Charlie; his went a bit faster but he was not as agreeable. Charlie kept pulling away and lifting his head out of my reach. He was aware of my carrot distraction and it didn't work with him but I managed to finish the job. I asked Denni not to laugh at my first attempt at making rope halters but his reply was that they would do the job, his way of saying that they weren't too bad. He trimmed the horses' hooves, telling me Charlie had hard hooves and Jonesy had been shoed before. I asked how much I owed him and he wouldn't charge me anything. I thanked him and gave him a hug. I had come to the realisation that there are two kinds of people in the Australian outback; the kind that will give you the shirt off their back if you asked. The other is one that would rather see you suffer and turn a blind eye then to help someone in need, and at times unfortunately go out of their way to make life that little bit more difficult for you. Thankfully, I came across more of the shirt off their back kind of people.

The caretakers of the Showground arrived and explained they were having cattle arrive and would be using the stables so I had to move. They suggested that they could arrange for me to stay at the Jondaryn Woolshed, which I gratefully accepted. I collected the lead ropes to the round paddock and led both horses to the stables. I put hobbles on Jonesy while he was there. I kept a close eye on him, as this was his first time wearing them. In the beginning, he wasn't happy and just stood still, then he moved around a bit and I opened his gate and let him out to eat grass. Charlie became jealous so I hobbled him and let him out too. Charlie wasn't interested in eating grass; instead he was more interested in attempting to take off, which he succeeded in. This startled Jonesy but thankfully, he just stood there, he didn't know what to do. Charlie was running around doing bunny hops and I tried to catch him, which only encouraged him more. I took Jonesy's hobbles off and walked him to the water trough, and Charlie followed thinking Jonesy was going somewhere interesting. I should have put the lead rope on Charlie and tied him up first because, when I took his hobbles off, he bolted. I grabbed some carrots, walked Jonesy to the round paddock, and put him in. Charlie followed but was not interested in going into the paddock, he ran around the outside instead. I followed holding out a carrot but Charlie wasn't to be distracted so I put the lead rope on Jonesy and opened the paddock gate. I led Jonesy into the middle of the paddock and started feeding him carrots. Charlie, hearing the crunching, walked into the paddock to get his share. I left them both eating carrots in the middle of the paddock and closed the gate. Finally, I felt I was one up on the horses. Morris arrived at dark and brought more of my things from his place and a bottle of wine and Joe joined us. Again, Morris pulled out his swag and slept over. In the morning, I brought the horses in from the yard and brushed them, cleaned their hooves and put easy boots on both of them.

The next few days were spent training and riding Jonesy. Charlie was introduced to the packsaddle, by itself first, then with bags, and then with the netting and bags. I soon discovered that Charlie took off when he is in hobbles and is too fast to catch (Morris thought Charlie needed his three legs hobbled but it sounded dangerous). Charlie looked so scary running in hobbles - he did bunny hops, with his front legs in the air and jumped with his back legs. To stop him, I led Jonesy in the opposite direction and fed him carrots. Charlie turned around real quick and followed Jonesy, not wanting to be left behind, or miss a snack. Jonesy tried running in hobbles however, after two steps he almost fell over, so he didn't try again which I was very relived about, he was also much more interested in eating grass than running around like crazy Charlie.

Joe has given me much advice on the horses and has helped me make a rope bridle for Jonesy. Helping me out with the problems with Charlie (trying to run ahead on our rides), Joe loaned me a rearing mouthpiece, a solid heart-shaped bit. The curves on top of the heart are placed in the horse's mouth and the bottom pointed bit came out under the chin. Joe's number one rule was that the horse must not be tied up with the bit in its mouth as it can break the horse's jaw. He demonstrated the bit on Charlie after I put the packsaddle on and some bags. He walked Charlie, the bags moved and Charlie started to go crazy so Joe tugged the lead rope attached to the bit and it drew him back in line. I was stunned as Charlie was about to do his 'bucking the bags off' routine and Joe stopped this. I couldn't wait to give it a go myself. I took Charlie out into the paddock and he was about to start bucking, but I brought him into a walk and calmed him down. He followed me and did everything I wanted, stopping and walking when told to, the bit worked amazingly well. Later, I took Charlie for a ride and he acted up as usual, but calmed down with the rearing bit in his mouth. I was riding Jonesy and leading Charlie with the empty packsaddle. He wanted to run ahead and nip at Jonesy, but with this rearing bit, I was able to keep control and get him to behave and walk properly.

My next step was training Charlie walking with the gear in the packsaddle and not to flip out when the bags moved or shifted. I'd been putting a few small bags on him while training, so it had not been too much of a problem, but when I had heavy bags it's another matter. It was difficult to do up the clasps and I needed both hands to clip the bags shut over the packsaddle. With Charlie moving about, this was impossible to do. I had finally finished training Jonesy. He was familiar with the hobbles, water bucket, how to lead Charlie, how to ignore annoying Charlie, and how to kick Charlie when he tried to nip his bum. Jonesy never ran away and always came to me when I approached. I had no problems with Jonesy. Charlie on the other hand needed more work and, for the first time, he chased Della out of the paddock. Della seemed to have enjoyed our practice walks and didn't tire, still full of energy when we returned. Jonesy and Charlie had both been good while on the road with Della, no aggression at all. They didn't seem to even notice Della, unless she stopped right in front of them. Even then, the horses continued walking steadily so I was surprised Charlie had scared Della enough to make her run out of the paddock. The saddlepad and packsaddle are fine for Charlie but he does avoid the bags when they are near him. One morning I brought both horses in from the round yard, saddled Jonesy and put the packsaddle and some gear on Charlie, strapping the gear on with stretch cords, just in case. However, I was full of confidence with both horses. I had my magic rearing bit! We headed out and it was all going well, Charlie was behaving and not going ahead. I thought this would be a pleasant trip to the Jondadyn Woolshed. I decided to put both reins in my left hand and hold onto Charlie's lead-rope with my right hand so when I gave Charlie instructions, it wouldn't confuse Jonesy. As I was doing this, the right rein slipped and fell to the ground. I said 'whoa', gently pulling back on the remaining rein. Jonesy turned to the left and stepped into long grass and that's when I noticed the barbed wire on the ground. In a split second, I knew what was going to happen - Jonesy bolted as soon as his hoof landed on the barbed wire. I had no control as I only had one rein. I fell off the backside of Jonesy and as I fell, I dropped Charlie's lead- rope. Since I had that second, I knew I would be falling and managed not to land too badly. I was able to stand up right away, but both horses were off down the dirt road. I had a sore knee but was able to walk. I started to follow them, and passed a house. The owner came out and pointed the way my horses had gone. He thought they'd be far away and asked if I wanted a lift. Della and I jumped into his ute and we headed off. We found Jonesy first - he was eating grass and a jockey from the Oakey Racetrack was holding his reins. I reluctantly explained that the horse belonged to me. The jockeys name was Phil, and he offered to look for my other horse, saying that Charlie had run down the dirt road and wasn't stopping for anything. Thanking him, I asked Phil to hold Jonesy's bridle as I mounted, as

I was still shaky from the fall and rode off down the road in pursuit of Charlie, *perhaps he'd gone to Jondaryn and then I won't have to lead him far I thought to myself.* Then I remembered the rearing bit - *oh my God* …it just hit me. Charlie could have stepped on the lead-rope and ripped his jaw off. I couldn't ride - I just started walking fast down the road, becoming very upset, crying and thinking about the pain it would have caused. Charlie would be bleeding, *that's why he took off like that*! I stopped every car that drove by and asked if they'd seen Charlie, my packhorse. 'Yes' everyone replied, 'they'd seen him and he wasn't slowing down. He was running full speed down the dirt road'. I just hoped he wouldn't cross the train tracks or the highway. Every person I asked said he was further away. Phil and Noel drove by in a white ute and said they would catch up to him. I explained about the rearing bit and that's why he'd bolted. They drove off ahead and I kept walking Jonesy. I just wasn't walking fast enough so I decided to hop back up on Jonesy and he decided to take off when I mounted. I held on but the stirrup broke and I fell off, landing hard. Winded, I couldn't move… couldn't breathe. Della was in my face, full of concern, but the last thing I wanted was her licking me. I grabbed her collar, pushed her an arm's length away from me, and held her there. I just concentrated on breathing. It took a while but finally I was able to get some breaths. I slowly stood up, both my arm and my knee hurt but I was able to walk. I looked around for Jonesy but he was nowhere to be seen. I continued walking down but it was hurting and I started crying, upset over Charlie and how he would be feeling. I also felt an overwhelming feeling of failure, all those negative remarks from people before I began this trip came flooding back. Maybe they were right, was this the most stupid idea I ever had, was I going to die out here? In the distance, a white ute came into view with my horse following behind. I was so relived they had found Charlie and he wasn't dead. I was also worried about the damage that would have happened when he'd stepped on his lead rope. As the ute pulled closer, I saw Phil was sitting in the back holding the lead rope with Charlie running alongside. They stopped and asked me what had happened to my riding horse. I explained I'd fallen off and he'd run into the nearby plowed field, so they went looking in the direction I had last seen Jonesy. As Noel drove the other ute back to his house, I sat in the back of the ute with Della and held onto Charlie's lead-rope. He was bleeding from the mouth, but his jaw wasn't dislocated. I was upset he was bleeding and thinking how much his mouth must be hurting. We passed the paddock Phil had caught Jonesy earlier, and there he was again, just hanging out in front of the horse paddock eating grass.

We stopped and I walked to Jonesy and grabbed his reins, now I had both horses but I was hurting badly. Noel felt sorry for me and invited me to rest at his place across the street. We walked the horses over to the stables and put them in separate stalls, tying them up so they wouldn't roll with their saddles on. I removed Charlie's bit and washed it in the water – it had blood on it. I tried to check Charlie's mouth but he wouldn't let me and kept lifting his head up out of my reach. I left him to soak his mouth in the water trough. I hobbled over to a nearby canvas chair and accessed my injuries. My knees were bruised but not bleeding, my upper left arm was hurting, the bruise already starting to show. My chest cartilage pain had returned so I took some painkillers and chatted to Noel and Phil, and found they ran a business breaking-in thoroughbred racing horses. What are the chances? After the painkillers kicked in, I resolved to walk the horses to the Jondaryn Woolshed instead of riding. The men wouldn't hear of it and insisted on loading us up on the float and driving us to Jondaryn Woolshed. They were so nice and I thought Phil was so good looking. *I wish Phil could come with me on the trip. Oh well, I'll never get a good-looking cowboy.* Noel helped unload the horses, we put them in the stables, and I tied them up. Inside the office, I paid for a bed in the shearer's quarters. I unloaded the horses and put them both in the paddock. Charlie hung out by the water trough keeping his mouth in it. I felt so bad. I was so wretched at causing him pain, I cried some more. Lucky dies, now Charlie is injured and that's my fault, 'because I didn't see the bigger picture. It just never crossed my mind that Charlie could get hurt with the rearing bit.

I went back to the shearer's quarters and laid down very depressed and upset with myself. When Morris arrived, he was upset with me and gave me a lecture but I told him I already felt guilty for the pain I'd caused Charlie. In Morris' ute we drove to the Oakey Showground to pick up my supplies. I left Joe a note in his shed, along with his rearing bit. We returned to Jondaryn and Morris had another go at me about what happened to Charlie. I felt so bad I went to bed early and cried myself to sleep. In the morning, Morris left to go town and I waited for the vet. She showed up and I had her look at Charlie's mouth. She gave Charlie a sedative to relax him so she could open his mouth and found two cuts on his tongue, injecting him with Bute - a painkiller. She explained cuts in the mouth heal quickly and these ones had already started healing and that Charlie didn't

Della's Destiny

need stitches. She said I could pick up some more bute, antibiotics, and tetanus injections from the clinic. When Morris returned, we were driving up to the vet to pick up Charlie's medicine when I received a phone call from Shayne (an AFL player) who informed me that he had arranged transport for us to Mitchell. I thanked him and we turned around to go back to the Jondaryn Woolshed to meet Rudd's Horse Transport. I organised my gear and was readying the horses when Mark pulled up in the float. I was ecstatic that the AFL Broadbeach, Old Boys, had arranged a float for us. I gave Morris a big hug goodbye ecstatic that we could continue our trip.

The horses loaded easily into the back, then Della and I climbed into the front. I had to pick Della up and lift her onto the floor of the front of the truck; it was so high off the ground. I climbed the three steps to get into the cab, which took a bit of effort with my injuries, but I managed. Then Mark, the driver, climbed in and we were on the road to Mitchell! Mark didn't mind me chatting, he was a bit upset about Della, but when he realised that Della isn't like most dogs, he was fine. Della just slept on the floor of the cab. Della didn't climb on the seat or bark, and she was very well behaved. I explained that Della is well behaved and never any problem, probably the most well behaved dog Mark had ever seen. He completely forgot she was in the truck and chatted awhile too as we exchanged our stories. It was dark by the time we arrived at the Mitchell Showground. We unloaded the horses and put them into separate stalls in the stables. We gave them buckets of water and hay. Mark went to take a shower and I set up my swag in the stables. It was dark and I couldn't see the layout of the grounds so I just went to bed and decided to have a look in the morning.

Mark loaded his horses early and left me my bale of hay I had brought along and two plastic water buckets. In the morning, I had a walk around, found the cattle yards and led the horses there to have a wander for the day. I then worked on making my 'Wanted: Adventurous Horsey Man Ad.' I walked to town and found a place to print the ad then took myself to the Great Artesian Spa to soak away my injuries. Later, I walked around Mitchell putting up the flyer.

The next morning I closed all the gates on the grassy arena in the middle of the Showground and led Charlie there to wander. I saddled Jonesy for a ride being very careful and thorough to make sure everything fitted where it should. I walked him around the Showground and let him have a 'sticky beak' and I kept my eyes open for any holes or anything that could make him spook. The grounds were fine but I was extra careful to make sure everything would go smoothly. Having followed all of Morris' rules, I mounted Jonesy. He took off like a rocket and, as I tried to pull him under, I fell off and hit the ground hard. It took a while but when I finally sat up, oh boy, the pain was incredible. I limped my way to my swag and supplies, pulled out my medical kit and began assessing my injuries. My face was pouring blood so I took care of that first, cleaning the gravel rash and applying some ointment to help stop the bleeding. My jaw felt dislocated and my ribs on the left side felt cracked - not that I could do anything about that, other than strapping them. Both of my wrists were sprained so I wrapped them in bandages. I couldn't work my fingers so I couldn't undo my jeans to look at my knees, so I left them. I limped over to get Jonesy who was eating grass by the side of the arena with Charlie. I led him over to the stables and took his gear off. Jonesy went into a stall and stayed there for the rest of the day. I gave him a bucket of water and I fed him hay. I waited for the painkillers to set in, so I could take off my jeans and change into shorts. My knees were bleeding so I took care of that and laid down to rest.

A few hours later, a lady called Belinda showed up at the Showground to collect manure for her garden. She took one look at my knees and asked if I needed to go to the hospital. I looked down at my knees and they were swollen - the left knee looked like a watermelon. I was shocked it had become so swollen since my knees didn't hurt as much as my face, jaw, chest and wrists. I declined and took more painkillers and lay down to sleep. I couldn't eat as my jaw was closed up tight so just drank water and swallowed tablets. The next day I tried eating but I couldn't chew. Therefore, I broke pieces of pop tarts, placed a piece in my mouth, and let it dissolve slowly and then I would swallow. At this point, I decided that horse riding was too unsafe and I just couldn't get back on again. I was hurt, sore, and knew my recovery from these injuries would take time. I also knew that it was a big risk to get back on the horses, if I fell again it could mean the end of the trip. While I was recovering from my injuries, Della explored the Showground and found an old kangaroo leg bone to chew on. Then Della spotted a goanna and this goanna was huge and didn't run up a tree to get away like all the other ones that Della had encountered before. This goanna stood its ground and Della was the loser in that standoff!

Della and the standoff

I began to think of other ways that Della and I could make it across Australia - ones that she would enjoy. I decided a bicycle might fit the bill. With a bicycle, I could go at a safe speed and it would be a shorter distance to fall off. *Not that I will fall off a bike, but knowing my coordination and injuries, I probably will.* Belinda showed up again for more manure and we talked. I told her I was selling Jonesy and she said that she would mention it to 'horsey' people in the area and offered me a lift to the spa to soak away my injuries. I accepted as I was limping badly and could barely walk. The spa had a hot natural healing pool and I soaked away my pain. As I was walking back to the Showground, Jeffery and his family pulled up and offered me a lift. We all chatted and they were interested in buying Jonesy. I was happy as I wanted to get rid of him, I didn't want to see Jonesy anymore. Gabrielle looked Jonesy over. She was a young girl but she knew her way around horses. Jeffery, her father, was very friendly and informed me that he was a kangaroo hunter. I was aghast when I heard that, but I didn't say anything. I know that people have different beliefs and lifestyles and I do my best to treat everyone the same and not judge them. Jodie, Gabrielle's mum, checked Jonesy over and proclaimed him a good horse. She asked if she could bring Dustin, their professional horse-riding son around the next afternoon to give Jonesy a ride. Friendly Jodie asked about my injuries and offered to drive me to the spa the following day.

The next morning, Jodie showed up right on time and I was ready. I soaked in the spa for a while, then lied down in a lounge chair and fell asleep until the place closed for lunch. After a shower and dressing I hobbled back to the Showground, I rested until the family showed up that afternoon. Dustin arrived bringing his own saddle, reins and a ute full of girls. Gabrielle and I caught Charlie and brought him up to the stables so I could brush him, while Dustin sorted out Jonesy. Dustin rode well and had no dramas with Jonesy. He tried to take off when Dustin mounted but Dustin, being a professional rider, kept him in line and declared Jonesy was fine, but he didn't need a horse but would let his mates know that Jonesy was available. Jeffery and Jodie said they were going to Roma on Tuesday and offered me a lift. I thanked them and told them I would think about it and give them a call. The next few days, I just rested, I didn't go into town, because I hated limping and it caused me more pain. The pain relief tablets made me sleepy, so I sent Jodie a text that we would take up her offer for a lift into Roma. The whole family showed up the next morning with a horse float, including the girls though Dustin wasn't there. We loaded my supplies into the back of the ute and the horses on the float. Della sat in the back with Gabrielle and during our trip I asked Jeffery about his job. He was the first kangaroo hunter I'd met and I enjoyed learning new things. Jeffery was very interesting and had lots of information and stories for me. I learned so much on that ride to Roma and wished the drive could have been longer but they dropped me off at the Roma Showground.

After we unloaded the horses, I tied the horses up per Morris' instructions, set my gear in a pile and thanked the family for all their generous help. I walked the horses down to the small paddock and tied Della up to the supplies. I walked to Toy World where Janelle, one of the owners, was very helpful and explained about the bicycles they had in stock. I asked about modifying a bicycle and installing a small 48cc petrol engine. Janelle replied that would be Chris' area of expertise and introduced me to Chris, another owner. Chris wasn't interested in bicycles motors, or my trip then I realised he was watching the Melbourne Cup Race on TV (which is much more important, if your an Aussie) so I left and went to the library where I printed off some information about the motor I wanted to buy and bicycle trailer. On the walk back to the Showground, I came upon a guy on a pushbike. He had been at the library earlier and I asked him where he'd bought his bicycle. We sat down in the park, had a chat about my trip, and discussed where I could find a bicycle. His name was Baz and he was very helpful and friendly. He told me a bit about himself. He said he couldn't go with me on the trip because he was on parole, but he said it sounded like a great trip. We exchanged numbers and agreed to see each other the next day. Della was happy to see me. While I was putting the horses in the large grassy padlock, the caretaker came by and said that I would have to leave on Monday, because the tent city was going up for the Roma Cup. I asked if I could set up my swag under the stables and the caretaker agreed.

I phoned Morris and asked if he could come and pick up the horses by Monday. Della and I could find a place to stay, but with horses, it would be hard to find a place. Morris agreed to come, get the horses, and take care of them. *What a nice guy, I owe him big time. I'm very grateful to Morris.* I set up my swag in a sheltered spot in the stables and went to sleep but rose early in the morning and sorted out the horses. I decided to take Della with me on our five-kilometer walk to the other side of Roma to visit D & K Motorcycles, another pushbike store. I talked to the owner but he wasn't keen to help me out about the engine, due to insurance regulations. He gave me Matt's address, explaining that Matt might be able to help me. So, Della and I walked back into town and found Matt's Small Engine Repair shop.

Chapter Six
Matt's Small Engine Repairs

Matt was an older, friendly, good looking bloke and one of the first things he said was that he has seen us in the Roma paper and he gave me the newspaper to keep. He seemed very keen to take on my project and I was happy to have found someone who was interested and willing to help. I had been feeling down about all the setbacks and accidents; however, Matt's enthusiasm had me excited again. Matt's cute son, Steven, who was friendly and talkative, arrived with some food, they had a break, and I showed Matt the information I had printed. Matt called the stores and ordered the bicycle trailer and the motor for me, having them delivered to his address. Then Matt called Chris at Toyland to order the bicycle and Chris said he would investigate. Della and I left and met Baz. During our talk, he said he would find me a bicycle to borrow while I was in town, so I wouldn't have to walk all the way from the Showground every day and he walked me to a Medical Clinic for some pain relief tablets. The doctor gave me several prescriptions and insisted I have x-rays done. I knew I didn't have broken bones, but the doctor wanted proof nothing was broken.

The next day Della and I walked into town and went to see Chris at Toyland about the bicycle. Chris was going out for a break and suggested I come back later, so Della and I went and visited Baz at the arts school where he worked. Once Della and I returned to Toyland, Chris informed me the bicycle that I was interested in was out of stock. If we were to order it today, there was a good chance it would take a few months to arrive at Chris's place. I patiently explained I didn't need that particular model, just a bicycle similar to that one; a 26inch man's steel frame, with front suspension only. Chris replied he would seek a bicycle like that and to come back the following day. I asked him about lights for the bicycle and he just pointed, saying 'over there'. Therefore, I looked at them by myself until Janelle approached me. She was very helpful, and explained the lights to me. I asked Chris if he thought the bicycles he had in the store would suffice, rather than having to order one in. Disinterest, he told me to read the tags on the bicycle to find out. I persevered and asked about a bicycle repair kit and saddlebag to put all our supplies in. Without taking his eyes off the TV, he pointed to the corner of the shop. I realised that Chris preferred sitting in the back of the store, watching horseracing rather than assisting a customer. He was better suited to working at the racetrack or a TAB than Toyland. Since Chris was too busy with horseracing to help, I decided to go to the library and use the Internet to look for a bicycle in nearby Dalby. I soon found I could order everything I needed over the internet and began printing bicycle information and took it to Matt. He looked it over and gave me his advice on what bicycle to buy, seat saddle, parts, lights, repair kit, and pannier racks. Della and I returned to the library to order everything Matt had recommended. While I was ordering from three different online stores, I thought to myself *Toyland is going to go out of business. Poor Janelle, Chris' 'No customer service' policy will drive the local people to buy from the Internet too.* Everything I bought was cheaper than Toyland and most of the places had free delivery.

I met up with Baz who informed me he had found me a black beaten-up bicycle to ride around town. I didn't care about the condition of the bike because I needed practice before my new bicycle arrived - Della would need the practice too. I used my riding horse helmet, as I hadn't yet bought a bicycle helmet. The bicycle had a very uncomfortable seat however; it was what I needed to get around town and worked fine. I went to visit Matt and asked Steven if he wanted to go to the movies on Friday night. He asked what was playing and we watched the preview of' Looper' on his phone and agreed to meet me at the movies. Riding the bicycle took me no time to get back to the Showground that night and I made it there before the rain started falling. The next day, I updated my diary while waiting for the rain to stop, riding into town on the bicycle with Della running alongside. My GPS showed we had averaged a speed of eleven kilometers an hour (the town was 2.5 kilometers from the Showground). We met Baz and he gave me a pair of bike gloves and a bicycle helmet. We figured with the trailer attached and after a few days of getting into shape, I should average ten kilometers an hour on the road. If I use the motor that can reach twenty kilometers an hour, swap pedals for motor every hour and ride for seven hours a day, I should average 100 kilometers a day. We visited Matt and saw Steven there. He said he would go home after work, have a shower and then meet me in front of the cinema. Later, I left Della with the locked-up bicycle, met Steven at the cinema, and enjoyed the movie. After the movies, Steven rode his bicycle, I rode my borrowed one and Della ran alongside us on the grass all the way back to the Showground. We ended the evening talking and watching music videos on my iPad. Steven left and rode home. I was hoping for a kiss but didn't even get a hug goodbye!

The next morning it rained and Della ran around getting muddy, wet and dirty. I rode into town and hung out with Baz at the art school. Baz arranged for me to have a room there and I rode the bike home with Della running alongside. I found she could run so much faster than I can and I'm on a bike. I kept yelling at her to slow down and wait for me. I think she just wanted to show off and reassure me that she will be able to keep up on our trip. After more researching on the Internet while tucked away in my warm swag at the Showground, I found an amazing website. www.cycletrailsaustralia.com. This website provided a lot of useful information for my transport style with lots of links to helpful websites. The next day was Sunday and Morris was coming over. I was so excited I brought the horses in from the back paddock and brushed them, prettying them for Morris, when Jonesy stepped on my left big toe. I guess Jonesy wanted me to give me something to remember him by, as if I could forget. I was still wearing pressure bandages on my knee and wrist from when he'd thrown me.

I cycled into town with Della and we visited Baz at the art school again. He informed me he would like to come on the trip with me and showed me the quality expensive mountain bicycle he'd just purchased. The bike had a rear pannier rack and headlamps. It seemed to me that Baz was getting serious, so we talked about what to bring and the route to take. My bicycle will have a trailer, front pannier-rack and a front-basket. The trailer will have room for Della when she gets tired but she is always so full of energy and I doubted that she would have any problems keeping up with the bike. I knew I would not be able to pedal very fast until I got my legs into bicycle racing form. I'd be struggling to get 50 kilometers a day on the bicycle and I know Della can do 100 kilometers and still have energy to run around the campsite and go swimming at night. Baz had one waterproof bag and wanted to buy three more saying they will fit on his rear rack. I thought two bags on each side would be too many and that he would have to have front racks too or just bring two bags. After lunch at the Arts school, I received the key to my room from Mick the landlord. Morris called saying he was on his way to Roma so Della and I left to go back to the Showground. The caretaker came past and I paid him for our stay. The other travelers I came across were having a Sunday session so I joined in and told them about my trip and Morris. Della and I waited at the front gates of the Showground to give Morris directions. I was feeling cheeky and happy to see Morris so when he pulled up in his ute, I lifted up my shirt and showed him my bra, he shook his head and laughed at me. I introduced Morris to the caravan campers and we went to look at the horses. We put them in the smaller pen for the night and then went to my swag and had a few drinks and chatted. Morris is taking my packsaddle for Pat so she can take fencing supplies up the mountain to fix her fence. I'm glad that the saddle will be put to good use and I liked to help. Pat wanted to pay for the saddle so I told her the cost would be $250 for the packsaddle and pack blanket, and I threw in the tail cropper, girths, and netting. I agreed Pat could pay in installments, I didn't mind about the money as I really liked Pat and so enjoyed the time I'd spent with her, but I could really do with the money, as my bank balance was low.

Morris says he would take the horses to the riding pens and give them a workout. He suggested I wait a few days to put Jonesy up for sale on the Internet. He wanted to get rid of Jonesy's 'taking off at full speed' action. Morris was tired and climbed into his swag early. I wanted to talk a bit more, so I crawled into his swag with him and had a cuddle. It was nice sleeping next to someone especially since it was a cold night. I was hoping Morris would make a move but he didn't. He wasn't a cowboy at all he was a proper gentleman. Morris had everyone fooled into thinking he was a cowboy, even me. Now I knew better! What did a girl have to do to get his attention? Morris got up around 4am to get some coffee but never climbed back into the swag when he returned from his coffee run, so I just got up and took a hot shower. It probably should've been a cold shower but it was still chilly out. He loaded my gear in the back of his ute and drove me to the arts school and we carried it up to my room before climbing back into his ute and driving to the Showground. We loaded the horses, Jonesy caused a bit of a drama while loading, but Charlie walked up the ramp with no worries at all. I hugged Morris as tight as I could (remember my bruised ribs) and kissed him goodbye. I knew I would miss Morris and the horses, but mostly Morris. I felt my eyes starting to water, but I stopped myself thinking about them leaving. I knew Morris would take good care of them and maybe I'd ride again someday. I wanted to keep Charlie though, taking him on walks, feeding him carrots and he could eat my grass so I didn't have to mow my acres with a push mower.

(*Back in Coraki my neighbors' think I'm crazy when they see me with my push mower, mowing three acres. I can never finish the job because the property is too big - I just do a section at a time. Sometimes one of the neighbors' will come over on his ride-on tractor and help. The neighbors' also think I am crazy when I took Lucky for walks. I don't care - he'd been stuck in the same old paddock every day and he always enjoyed his walks - he loved to have a sticky beak and smell things.*)

Watching Morris's ute and float drive away I felt so sad, that part of my life was over. I wondered if I'd ever be horse-obsessed as I once was or whether the damage from the last fall, had scarred me for life. I hoped one day I'd be able to trust a horse to ride again but at that moment, nothing could have convinced me to mount a horse again. *Perhaps, spending time with Charlie, as I used to do with Lucky, will cause me to change my mind.* I said goodbye to the caravan neighbors and hopped on the pushbike, riding into town with Della running on the grass beside me. We went to our new accommodation at the arts school and Della had a fenced in area in the backyard to stay in - I set up and organised her sleeping mat, bucket of water and food dish there before going to visit Matt. Smiling Steven was there with his cute dimples looking excited. My trailer had arrived. He was opening the box and we put the trailer together, it was smaller than I thought it would be. I wanted it to be taller so the bags wouldn't fall out. I went round town looking for materials to make it taller (Matt called it 'greedy bars'). I finally found the aluminum and glass store, it had just what I needed, but they were closing shop for the day. So Della and I returned to the arts school for the night and first thing in the morning, we headed back to the store. They cut the rods to our specifications and I carried the supplies to Matt's and waited for Steven to come back from his smoko. We worked on the trailer during his breaks and after he finished work, we had a drink and completed the trailer. Della didn't like the trailer in the beginning; however once she became tired from all the running she would soon see the trailer as a resting place. The trailer looked great and I was very happy with it; Steven had done a terrific job. I stuck many reflectors on the back so everyone would see me on the side of the road. I also saved a spot for the flashing/steady five LED red lights to go on the top rail. Della and I walked back to the arts school and Baz had sent me a text explaining all the equipment he had purchased for the trip. Mudguards were a highly useful item according to the bicycle touring websites, so I ordered some on the Internet. Baz came back from Camping World with a bag full of supplies and I went to the library to put Jonesy for sale on 'Gumtree' and check my tracking status of the things I had ordered as no bicycle or parts had arrived. The next few days were all about the bike. I'd received an email from Big W - they'd changed the delivery date to the following week. I was very upset and called them but was informed they could not speed up the delivery as it was already in the freight company's hands. I walked to Matt's to deliver the bad news and he suggested I cancel the order and get a bicycle from elsewhere. I called Big W again and tried to cancel the order but they informed me that they couldn't cancel the order as it was on its way. When I told Matt, he said 'act assertive - they changed the delivery date on you and you have every right to cancel and have a full refund'. The third time calling Big W, after yelling, threatening, and swearing they finally agreed to give me a refund and cancel the order. I was so worked up and upset after that phone call. I don't like having to yell and swear in order for them to take me seriously. It put me off Big W for life.

Then it was back to the Internet at the library looking for a bicycle that would fit the Zbox engine. After a while, I realised most mountain bikes have large lower bars in the frame and I wouldn't find one that would fit the engine. So, I called Zbox to ask what I should do and they explained that there was an adaptor in the box they shipped to us that would fit larger frames. I was excited about that news that Della and I ran back to Matt's to have the Zbox guy explain to Matt the good news and he was happy about that. I then ran to Toy World and bought their only steel frame mountain pushbike, a blue 20-inch steel frame, 26-inch tires, 36 spokes, Cheetah Kaktus. As it was the only one in stock, I was able to get it for the carton price. It was fully assembled which was a bonus that saved me $20. I was glad Chris wasn't working that day, just Janelle and her dad. I was so happy I'd finally had a bike. I gave Janelle's dad a hug and a kiss on the cheek. He told me I could bring the bike back anytime for free adjustments. I rode it to Matt's and read the instructions aloud while the rear sprocket of the engine was installed and then I fitted the new seat saddle myself. It was after 5pm and I didn't want to make Steven work overtime so I said we could work on it the next day but before he left, he installed the red rear 5 LED light onto the back of the trailer.

Baz showed up the next day with my rear bicycle rack. I walked to Matt's to drop the rack off, Steven had my bike on the worktable, and Matt was working on the engine chain. The motor, handgrip, and mudguards were all fixed to the bike; it was all coming together now. I dropped off the rear rack and left, as I knew I would constantly be asking questions and get in their way. I called Steven later and they had started the engine, put the front and rear pannier racks on, and were trying to figure out how to attach the trailer. I said I'd stop by the next day, which was Saturday, around 10:30am and see if it was ready to be tried out. I was sure Steven wanted to be the first around the block with it. I didn't mind he deserved first go since he had worked so hard on putting the bicycle and trailer together for me. Baz stopped by the Arts Centre, we talked about the trip, and I informed him of my research before deciding to go to the cinema and see Twilight - Breaking Dawn Part 2. Steven called to say he'd finished the bicycle and taken it for a test run and it went well. I asked about the bill as I was very short of funds and he replied that labor was $88 an hour and two mechanics had worked on it for four hours. I had no idea it would be that expensive and became very worried. I still owed for the trailer and motor, which was over $500. I only had $610 and $200.00 tied up on that Big W cancelled order.

Della and I walked to the shop next day and I checked the finished bicycle. It looked great but I still stressed about the invoice that was attached. I saw the total - $1,069.20. Nervously I asked Matt if I could pay $600 then, and $200 later when the Big W refund came through, paying the remainder on November. 28th, when Pat's payment for the packsaddle came through. Matt agreed and I was ecstatic. *I can take the bicycle today and be on the road again.*

Matt and Steve with Della in front of their shop

Matt adjusted the bicycle seat and handlebars and attached the red basket on the rear. I fastened the headlight on the bike and Matt showed me how a hose clamped worked and how to clean the air-filter. Time to take it away at last; Steven rode next to me on his bike and instructed me on how to start the engine. It was easy to do, except the clutch lever was hard to operate. Squeezing the lever hurt my wrist and hand that still hurt from falling off Jonesy. I managed to roll the trailer on the first turn, but it was empty and I now knew I had to take it easy on turns. I felt much more confident on the bike than the horse. I thanked the boys and asked Steven to come over later for a visit. I wish Steven could come with me. He would know how to fix my bike if something went wrong and he's really easy on the eye. Ah well, a girl can dream. I tied Della in the trailer and pedaled back to the arts school. I went slowly and Della didn't try to climb out. She would rather have run alongside, but I was in town and I didn't want to have to watch her, the traffic, and pedal the bike. It was easier with Della in the trailer. When I returned to my room, I packed everything, ate lunch, and fed Della. It started raining, so I put the bicycle under the school building so it wouldn't get wet, made a shelter for Della and waited for Baz. When he arrived, he explained that he would have to wait to collect his wages but I couldn't wait. I seemed to be continually pulled back to Roma every time I tried to leave. I needed to get away so we agreed he would catch me up in his ute and bicycle and meet me at the house his mother owned in Tambo.

Chapter Seven

New Start

My alarm went off at 2am. My body didn't want to get out of bed but thoughts of the open road lured me to get up and take a shower. I hadn't practiced loading the bicycle, so I did the best I could in the dark. It was so over-loaded I could see I would need to need to ditch a few things and sort it out in daylight. We set off at 4am. My cable-tied flashlight on the handlebars wasn't very bright, so I used my headlamp too. Della ran alongside and she had no problems keeping up. I pedaled slowly because the trailer was heavy and I didn't yet have my 'bicycle' legs. When the sky turned grey, we took a break and I tied the swag onto my backseat basket so Della could fit in the trailer. It was a pleasant cool morning and I wore my drover jacket and put Matt's safety vest over the top. Matt had given me the vest, its bright reflective strips ensured I could be seen in the dark but the road was lifeless and I didn't see a truck till after 5am, even then only three vehicles passed in the next hour. Traffic picked up after 8am, but since it was Sunday, it wasn't busy. It felt good to have the road all to ourselves. Live kangaroos and emus scampered around but the road kill continued. It was so sad and passing the smelly decomposing animals along the side of the road. It made me pine for the stock route, where we'd only seen live animals. With the roads so quiet, it was nice to pedal along and when I tired, I used the engine on hills and long flat stretches. When the road was downhill or a short flat stretch I would pedal. The engine took ten minutes to get cold when we took our breaks but we needed plenty, my bum and palms hurt. The first day we covered ninety-two kilometers and we averaged 15.6 kilometers an hour. We stopped and I took pictures at Muckdilla, Amby, and the Mitchell town signs. In Amby, I called Smokey, the drover, to see if he was home and pedaled over to join him for morning tea.

Smokey had mates helping him rebuild his house after the floods and we sat around chatting, telling me to watch out for snakes and spiders. I ended up falling asleep in the chair because I was so tired. I woke up around 1pm and Smokey advised me to camp at the Mitchell Weir. It had cooled down so we left and took advantage of the nice breeze. On the way to Mitchell, we had our first bad car driver who drove by and beeped his horn, almost forcing me off the road. That day, the other vehicles had driven in the far lane giving me plenty of room. It wasn't like there was any other traffic on the highway. I guess there will always be rude drivers. I avoided going off the roadway because of the bike's trailer. I didn't want it to tip Della out or to frighten her, her safety being my number one priority. When we arrived at the Mitchell Weir, I thought we'd gone to heaven it was so lovely. Luscious green grass, a splendid wide river, sheltered picnic tables, toilets and a BBQ, I could've stayed here forever! I quickly swapped my clothes for (I didn't pack a swim suit, I swam in boxer style underwear and a sports bra) my water shoes.

We walked down to the boat ramp and into the river – the cold felt so refreshing that Della and I swam to the middle and stayed in there for a long time. The sun shone and everything seemed ideal. We walked back to our supplies and bike and I cooked dinner and fed Della hers. Exhausted, I was in the swag happily sleeping by 6pm. We just loved being on the road and seeing new things. It had been a perfect day.

Next morning was an early start and everything went well. I made Della a larger space in the trailer so she would have more comfort. At our first rest stop I taught Della, who is a quick learner, to climb in the trailer by herself, she'd already figured how to get out. We'd seen lots of kangaroos and emus that morning with Della hanging her head out the passenger side of the trailer and watching the wildlife. We made it to the Mungallala rest stop where we had a break. We were planning to go for a swim in Morven, and continued along for about ten kilometers after leaving Mungallala; I was turning off the engine when I heard a loud bang. It sounded like a backfire from the engine. I stopped and dismounted to have a look. Slime was everywhere, all over the bike, Della, me, and the supplies - the rear tire and tube had blown right out. Baz had the tools and spares and he wasn't with me so I had no choice but to push the bicycle and walk. After a couple of kilometers, it was hot and I was getting tired, as the bike was so heavy with the trailer attached. I decided to wave down the next car that came along. Jason, in a large SUV, stopped and offered to take us into Morven. Unfortunately, he didn't have a wrench to unscrew the trailer and it wouldn't all fit in his SUV while still attached so, when another ute came along, I waved and a lady stopped. She had the tool we needed and we disconnected the trailer from the bike. She offered to put the trailer in the back of her SUV and drive it to Morven. Della and I climbed into Jason's vehicle and followed her into Morven. We stopped at the petrol station and discovered that there was no mechanic or bike shop in town. Jason was on his way to Augathella and offered to put the trailer in his SUV and drop us off there. So, I happily accepted the lift. Jason drove to the mechanic shop in Augathella but they had no bicycle tires or tube in the size needed.

I had finally got hold of Baz on my phone and he assured me that he would come by that night and bring the supplies. When I told Jason, he found me a great spot to camp by the Warrego River and wait for Baz. When we unloaded all my stuff from the car, it was sweltering so I decided to go for a swim with Della and invited Jason along. We soaked in the river for a while and talked. It was cold but refreshing. After the swim, Jason drove to the shops and arrived back with lunch, chips and Powerade. He gave me a can of spray oil for my bike chain and he left to continue on to Charleville. Della and I took a nap under the shady trees by the river. I talked to Baz a few times and he assured me that he was coming. I wasn't convinced. Baz was supposed to start out on this trip with me and he didn't. If Baz doesn't show up tonight, I will go to the mechanic shop tomorrow and see if they will order a bike tube and tire for me. I focused on the positive, I met the lovely Jason, my rescuer, and I had a pleasant spot to camp, with drinking water, a river to swim in and shade. It's a very quiet area on the river and no one drives down the Old Tambo Road. That night, while in my swag, with the cover down and the mesh zipped tight against the mozzies, I saw headlights coming down the road. It was 2am and knew it had to be Baz. I bounded out of the swag and sure enough, it was him. He explained that a huge kangaroo had jumped in front of his ute and he tried to stop, but it was too late. While he was checking on the kangaroo, another kangaroo jumped into the side of his ute, then bounced over it. There was nothing he could do for the kangaroo he'd hit and the ute hadn't fared well either. He'd ripped off the remainder of his mangled front-grill then looked under his bonnet and found his radiator was damaged. He managed to fix it sufficiently to finish the drive to pick me up and drive us to Tambo. We spent the night at his mother's unoccupied house in Tambo. Della and I had a room with a proper bed all to ourselves.

In the morning, I didn't wake Baz because he had driven all night. I unloaded my bicycle, trailer and the supplies from the back of his ute, watched some YouTube videos and read instructions on how to change rear tires, before calling Zbox and Matt with the questions I had. It took me five hours, but I finally finished changing the rear tire. I was very proud of myself, but I owed a huge thanks to Zbox and an even bigger thanks to Matt for the invaluable advice. Baz also helped me guiding the completed fixed tire onto my bike. Holding the tire and putting two chains back into their correct position was a little hard for one person. I gave Baz a big thank you for supplying the thorn-proof tires and the new tubes and spent the rest of the day taking tires and tubes off Baz's extra bicycles. I needed the practice; I didn't want to get another flat tire and spend four hours on the side of the road. Gradually I improved and decreased the time to under an hour, becoming far more confident regarding a flat tire. We packed our bikes and had pasta and beans for dinner, before heading to bed for a 3am start. In the morning, we had a hot drink and finished loading the

Della's Destiny

last of our things. Baz had a ten-liter can of water on the back of his bike and I thought that was over doing it as water was available along the route, but Baz wanted to be sure. He headed off before me whilst I finished the last-minute loading. I pulled away from the back porch and the trailer tipped over. Della wasn't in it and it was off balance so I pulled the trailer upright again. As I started down the road, I saw Baz walking his bike towards me. At first, I thought he was coming to check on me because I had taken so long but alas, his rear rack had broken and was sitting on top of his rear tire. I knew that heavy water jerry would be too heavy I thought. We hadn't even started and Baz's bike was unusable. Baz pointed out that my own trailer wheel-axle was bent. I panicked and had Baz hold my bike upright, while I checked the trailer wheel. I put some effort into it and straightened the wheel, hoping it held. I knew I would have to take extra care pulling the trailer.

I said sad goodbyes to Baz and continued. It was a perfect day for traveling, cool with lots of cloud cover. The road to Blackall was pleasant and we stopped at the rest stop 22 kilometers north of Tambo for a break. A guy pulled up and called out my name, it was Baz's neighbour, with a bag of tools for me. Baz had put together a bicycle tool-repair kit for me; we both knew I would need them in the future. The guy was friendly and we had a chat, and he offered a lift to Blackall but I was fine pedaling. He headed off, I finished my hot chocolate, and we continued on our way. As we went along, I would yell 'Look' to Della and point as masses of kangaroos and emus ran around - great herds of them. She would look out of the trailer and watch them as she loved watching the animals, even cows. She didn't bark at them, she just let her tongue hang out and wagged her tail. A Tambo police car stopped and asked if we were okay. The policeman was going to Blackall to get the police car serviced and we chatted before going our separate ways. Approaching a grid with a sign that said 'dog barrier fence', Della and I dismounted and pushed the bike around the gate. We stopped at a picnic area by the Barcoo River, Della went for a swim, and I took my shirt off and dipped it in the river to cool down. After a while, we decided to continue on to Blackall. As we rode along, we came across a guy on the side of the road. He was putting together a quote for fixing the road. We stopped and had a chat with him and he took our picture and filled up our water bottles with cold water. We rode on and there were road works. One lane was closed but the traffic controller said I should continue and they would hold the traffic on the other side until I passed through. I thanked him and off we went. When we arrived to the other side of the construction site, all the road workers, around twenty of them, were lined up, waving as we went by.

We came into Blackall and I found the campsite by the Barcoo River. Della and I went for a swim then I set up the swag and made dinner. I removed the trailer from the bicycle with the tools that Baz had given me, left Della with the gear while I pedaled into town, and filled up with two liters of petrol at the Caltex Station. On the way back the kill-switch on the engine stopped working so I pulled into a tire store and asked if they could help. They referred me to the mechanic down the street. I went there but he was most unhelpful so I called Matt to see what the problem might be. Matt explained that it would take two minutes to fix - it was simple and to let him talk to the mechanic so I put him on to him.

After the phone call, the mechanic said he could fit me in next Wednesday. I gave up in disgust and left the shop. On the way back to the campsite, I stopped to wash the dishes and fill up our water bottles. A man called Robert Stockwell pulled up in a white SUV and we had a chat, I mentioned about the hopeless mechanic and Robert told me that the locals see Derick Cooper at the Caltex Garage. Robert looked at the time and called Derick, asking him to stay back to have a look at my bicycle as I was on my way. I pedaled straight over and Derick fixed the problem in two minutes flat. *What a genius!* He didn't charge me and I was so happy I gave him a hug. Robert asked if he could have our picture for the local newspaper so Della and I went for another swim and then readied ourselves for the picture. Robert also autographed a picture book that he had published and gave it to me. It was filled with lovely photos of Australia. That night we hit the swag early.

We rose at 3:30am and were on the road as the sky turned grey and the road was pleasant. There was no traffic other than three very full kangaroo hunters' utes which passed us between 5am - 6am - dead kangaroos dangling from the metal racks. At our first stop, I tried to tighten the trailer on the bike, but just didn't have enough strength so we continued on, hoping everything would hold. Robert pulled up in his SUV, wanting to take some action shots so I dismounted and walked the bicycle around the first grid - Robert said we could ride over it but I worried about getting a flat tire. At the next grid, the gate was so far down along the fence-line, I decided to give the cattle grid a go. I lifted the bike over the grid and the trailer bounced along behind. Della, of course walked over the grid and it went fine - no flat tire.

Bicycling with Della in the trailer

Robert followed behind us for about twenty kilometers taking pictures, and then he thanked us and went on his way. I was happy to go over the grids, instead of pushing the bike around and through the gates since some of the gates were over a kilometer from the road and there seemed to be cattle grids every ten kilometers. As we went along, the bike began making a clinking sound. I thought it was from the engine chain hitting the mudguard, so I removed the metal mudguard. A bit farther down the road, the engine chain fell off so I replaced the chain. I noticed the trailer bolt was loose, so I tightened that as best as I could. One hour later the whole chain froze and I didn't even have the engine on. It was very hard pushing and thankfully at that moment a ute passed by and I waved them down. The ute pulled over and the three guys inside checked my bike. They asked for my tools and five minutes later, they had the bicycle fixed. One guy lifted the back of the bike, while the other two slipped the tire back into the correct place, tightened the nuts on either side and adjusted the de-railer. The rear tire had dropped out due to the jerking of the trailer bolt not being tight enough. Happy days again I had no worries with the bike after that.

We arrived at Conway Creek where I planned to camp the night. We walked down to the creek and it was filled with smelly green water. A dead calf that probably became bogged in the mud and couldn't get out filled the tiny mud-hole. I kept Della away I didn't want her getting sick from drinking that muddy water. We were hot, sweaty and craving a swim as we sat under the trees. I consulted the stock route map for the next water hole. We each drank a bottle of hot water, how we missed cold drinks. I decided to hit the road again in the hope that the next creeks would be water-filled. The breeze from cycling helped to cool us and Della hung her head out the side of the trailer to get the full effect. I just couldn't understand why it was so hot. I'd checked the weather yesterday and the highest was supposed to be 38 Celsius. We took breaks every half hour, sheltering under trees and drinking water. The next water point was 1.5 kilometers off the road and I didn't want to walk all that way in case it had dried up. The windmill in the distance didn't even have blades, so it seemed that point wouldn't have water either. We continued and saw cattle yards off the side of the road. How exciting, they had water troughs and an undercover area! We pulled up and Della jumped into the water trough before I had time to unbutton my shirt to dunk it in the water. I knew she needed a swim. Della soaked in the water trough for ten minutes whilst I sat on a barrel under the roof. I wet my bra and put it on and my wet shirt went on my head. It was 2pm - the hottest part of the day. We had another twenty kilometers left to Isisford and the Barcoo Weir campsite but I didn't care. We sat, rested, and stayed cool. Della jumped in the trough again and I dunked my shirt in the water when it started drying. A grey car pulled up and a lady got out and asked if we needed anything. I replied we were fine just having a break. She gave me a cold coke and a cold bottled water. I thanked her so much, a cold drink was just what I needed and the warm water wasn't refreshing. She asked if she should send the boys back in the ute to pick us up suggesting we stay at the station for a few days. It sounded tempting, but I declined. She told me to be careful, as it was 40 Celsius. After resting we set out again and took breaks every thirty minutes, resting in the shade from trees. It was too hot to eat - the heat just took our breath away. We finally arrived at Isisford at 4:30pm. We had been traveling for twelve hours, including breaks. I parked the bike and went into a shop asking for directions to the camping area. The shopkeeper directed me across the street, to the Council offices. Walking in from the heat, the chill hit me and the cold air-conditioning made me gasp so I had to sit down in the chair at the counter. The council lady asked me if I had heatstroke. I replied I was fine but was looking for the camping area. The council ladies were concerned and brought me two glasses of cold water. I couldn't understand their directions and had trouble comprehending what they were saying. After several attempts, I was still confused so they gave me a map of the town pointing out the camping spot, the showers and the swimming hole. All I was interested in was going to the Weir and swimming with Della. I thanked them and left. After finding the campsite, the first thing we did was park the bike and went swimming.

The water was warm in some spots, but where there was a current, it was icy cold and very refreshing. I set up camp, fed Della, and laid down in the swag, I was over tired and hungry but I didn't want to eat. Della on the other hand ate three bowls of dog food instead of her usual one. I finally ate a packet of instant noodles, to keep my stomach from growling and went to sleep. I woke up at 4am with horrible leg cramps, took another sleeping tablet and went back to sleep.

The next day Della and I spent all day swimming in the Weir. Jeff, a bloke who was staying at the camping ground, showed me his Camp 6 map and we figured out what rest areas we could stay at on our journey. Jeff traveled in a motor home with two birds. One of the birds talked and said 'what are you doing?' That's all it knew to say and the bird said it over and over. It became annoying after a while but the birds were friendly and cute and are lucky that they get to travel and see Australia. I wouldn't like to be a bird in a cage, kept in the same room my whole life it would drive me crazy! Della and I walked to the shower block then went back and tried to sleep, but all I did was sweat. After some time I gave up and went for a swim with Della. I hung the tarp to block the sun from the hitting the swag, but I still couldn't sleep it was just too hot. I went for another swim, and again lay down but sweat just poured off me - it was so uncomfortable and I didn't fall asleep till well after sunset. I woke at 2am to pack and hit the road. We were on our way to the 12 Mile rest stop. The council ladies had assured me there was a picnic shelter and a dam full of water there. The bike went perfectly all day, no breakdowns. The handlebars did slip a bit sideways, but I took out an Allen key and straightened them. We saw dozens of kangaroos they jumped across the road and Della became excited and started barking. I let her out of the trailer to have a run and she raced down the grassy side of the road and the kangaroos disappeared into the bush but she knew not to go chasing after them. We were pushing the bike over a grid when a car pulled up next to us. The guy stated we had to be keen to go biking in this heat and I agreed, assuring him we were going to stop for the day at the next rest stop. He continued on to Longreach and we went on our way to the 12 Mile rest stop and dam, only one other car passed us on the road that entire morning. When we came to a sign saying 'picnic shelter 300 meters' with an arrow pointing, I looked in the direction of the arrow and my heart jumped with joy, there was a windmill with all the blades and it was turning in the wind! I pulled onto the dirt road and pedaled to the picnic shelter. I parked the bike, using bungee cords around the frame, strapping it to a tree, took my shorts off and put my water shoes on. Della and I hightailed it to the dam - we walked across a cattle grid, climbed over a wire fence, up the embankment and as we looked over the crest, I saw the dam. It had lots of water in it! *Oh happy days!* Della dashed straight in and I was just behind her. The water was refreshing, not too cold or too hot - just right. In the middle of the dam, there was a white ball floatation device. I swam out to it, put the ball under my chest and just floated, watching Della swim around. After a while, we went back to the shelter and I put up the tarp to block the sun and erected the swag. Della went on the leash under the picnic table to sleep - I didn't want Della running around loose, because the council ladies had told me the previous day that dingo poison had been distributed. I was afraid if I took a nap, Della would wander around and find some to eat. I know

Della wouldn't run away or get lost I just wanted to keep her nearby and away from the poisoned meat.

I climbed into the swag with my wet clothes on and had a great nap. Della woke me up as someone was approaching. I unzipped the swag and sat up and found it was the guy in the car that morning who'd said I was keen. He'd brought me a 1.5-liter of icy cold Mt. Franklin water. We had a bit of a chat and I thanked him for his kindness before he left. I couldn't go back to sleep, so we had another swim before I climbed back in the swag with wet clothes and fell asleep. I had been feeling so tired and drained and I didn't know why. Maybe it's because I haven't had any fresh veggies or fruit in over three weeks. The dehydrated stuff just doesn't do it after a while and I just don't want to eat anything. I thought about the last few days, my symptoms, how I was feeling and concluded, I might have had a mild case of heatstroke. I woke up feeling hot so we walked down to the dam and watched two blokes putting out yabbie traps. I went into the dam, swam to the white ball, and had a chat with them. They said they would come back later to check the traps and drove off in their car. We had a very long soak and this time Della swam around for a while before swimming up to me. She looked tired, so I placed the floatation ball under her belly and wrapped my legs around the chain to hold it steady and she was able to rest in the water too. I put my arms around her and rested my chin on her back and she rested her head on my shoulder. We stayed like that for a long time. It was the hottest part of the day and we didn't want to get out of the water. Suddenly, Della lifted her head and perked her ears forward, and I turned to see what grabbed her attention. An adult emu, with seven medium sized chicks, was walking to the water hole for a drink. We stayed as still as we could, in the middle of the dam, and watched them all wade in and drink, then wander away. We rested on the white ball and watched to see if anything else would come by and it did. On the other side of the dam, another adult emu with three tiny baby chicks walked up, but before they got to the water, some birds started swooping and the adult emu hurried the baby chicks into the bush, so they didn't get a drink. We waited for a long time, hoping they would return but they didn't. I started getting a cold and shaky so we swam to the shore and went to the shelter. Now my hands were blue and wrinkly and I made a cup of hot chocolate to warm me up. Della lay in the hot dirt and took a nap.

In the late afternoon, we went for another long soak and I was hoping to see kangaroos appear for a drink. There are lots of kangaroo droppings around so I knew they came here for water. We waited in the middle of the dam again and this time we saw a different adult emu with five various sized chicks. I thought maybe this emu's chick-sitting for her mates. That group wandered away and we waited a little longer but the clouds covered up the sun and we began to get a chill so we went back to the shelter. I folded up the tarp and began to pack things away, so we would be sorted in the morning. Morris texted me and said he'd be arriving in Longreach the next day. I was excited at the prospect of seeing him again and answered that I would l be arriving the same day. Around 5:30pm, I decided to take another dip in the dam. Della and I wandered down to the waterhole and wallabies and kangaroos surrounded it. We startled them when we approached the water and they all ran away. We went for a swim and again quietly waited in the middle of the dam on the white ball. Della became bored with waiting and wanted to swim after the fish that were jumping out around us, but I asked her to wait and explained that it would be a lot more fun than trying to swim after fish. We had to wait over forty minutes, but it was worth the wait. They started coming one at a time, and soon wallabies and kangaroos surrounded us. Some had joeys, some went swimming, some just drank water and some joeys crawled out of their doe's pouch. We were turning in a slow circle looking and watching. Della was so good, she didn't bark, she just looked too. The animals kept coming and coming and I wished I'd had a waterproof camera I could have taken some great pictures! Twilight came and it was time to walk back to camp, otherwise we wouldn't be able to find our camp in the dark. As we swam towards shore, the startled animals didn't know what to do. They stopped doing what they were doing and stared at us. It was so funny they had no idea that we'd been in the middle of the dam. They were so busy looking behind them for danger that they never looked in the middle of the waterhole! The animals were bemused they just stood still. Della reached the shore first and two small wallabies near her ran away. The others just backed up and stared. When I stood up and climbed out of the dam, the animals on that side quickly took off. The ones on the other three sides continued to stare and we quickly walked up the embankment and left them to finish their drinking.

We went back to the camp, packed up, and went to sleep. The next day we had an easy pack and had a great start to the morning. The kangaroos were out in droves I had to pedal slowly to let them cross the road. I didn't want any of them hopping into the side of my bicycle or Della's trailer. We were doing well until we ran out of fuel. I hadn't realised how much I depended on that little engine. I pedaled for a while, but the wind was coming in from the north and blowing us backwards. The bicycle began to go so slow it was ready to tip, so I dismounted and had Della walk against the strong wind. I pushed the bicycle for five kilometers with Della walking beside me. It was a very quiet road and only two cars passed that morning. By the time we arrived at Ilfracombe, I was a hot and sweaty mess and it was only 6am. Pushing a bicycle and trailer against the strong wind was a huge effort. I pedaled through town, hoping to find a petrol station. There was none, but there was a petrol pump on the side of the road next to a closed cafe. The pump had a padlock on it so I figured, if someone took the effort to lock it, it must be working and have fuel. I parked the bike in front of the pump and went to knock on the house door, located behind the cafe. When no one answered, I went back to the bike and collected the fuel can. We walked to a house down a side street and knocked on the door and a very sleepy lady answered. I apologised for the early Sunday morning wake up, and explained our situation. She informed me that the cafe opened at 7am on Sunday and I could get fuel then. I thanked her and left. We walked back to the bike and I checked the time was 6:30am. I didn't want to have to wait till 7am, knowing the temperature was rising. I peered in through the glass doors of the cafe and spotted a man in the kitchen. I knocked, but he didn't hear me. I walked around and tried the side door and it was unlocked, so I walked in and explained the situation to the cook. He retrieved the key, walked to the pump and unlocked it; watching me put fuel in the can with the oil mix, and then dumped it into the tank. I bought two litres of fuel and he asked if I want to fill up the can again but I explained I was only going to

Longreach and wouldn't need fuel after that. I paid and thanked him for unlocking the pump early for me.

Outside I filled up the water bottles from the tap in the park and started for Longreach with Della in the trailer. This highway had many road trains and was extremely busy. The back routes had spoiled us where we had the whole road to ourselves. The road trains drivers were good and pulled over into the far lane when they passed us but they threw up rocks, dirt, and caused a huge slipstream of wind that almost blew us right off the road. It was a Sunday morning and we just couldn't believe how busy that road was. I thought it would've been quiet on a Sunday morning. Some road trains had four enormous trailers attached and they swung back and forth across the road when they pulled into the far lane. I started to seriously rethink the bicycle method of transportation. Neither Della or I were having fun on this highway, we cringed every time a road train barreled by. There was no live wildlife to be seen and the noisy road stank of dead road kill. We were only on the highway for twenty-six kilometers until we reached Longreach but we hated it. I wished there were back roads all the way to Western Australia and decided to do some more research regarding this. I felt unsafe and, instead of Della hanging her head out the side of the trailer and looking for animals as she usually did, she was curled up in a ball at the bottom of the trailer with her head under her paws. I felt horrible that Della wasn't happy. The handlebars kept slipping sideways, so I pulled off the highway and used the wrench and fixed them as best as I could. The bars still moved a little, I guess I just didn't have enough strength to tighten them properly. When we arrived in Longreach, I pulled over to take Della's picture in front of the huge 'Welcome to Longreach' sign.

Arriving in Longreach, QLD

We continued through the town. Longreach seemed quite a big town although we didn't stop as it was getting hot and I knew Della wanted to go for a swim. Back on the highway to Winton, we passed the farewell sign for Longreach and about four kilometers out of town came across the Apex River Park. We took a right and Della jumped out of the trailer when I walked across the cattle grid pushing the bike. She didn't want to get back in and ran on the grass alongside the bicycle until we found the campground area next to the river. I bungee tied the bicycle to a tree and walked Della down to the big river. Della was so excited about going for a swim, that she didn't even notice the two chickens running around. There were quite a few utes with boat trailers on the side of the road which made me aware this place was a popular boating spot.

We walked back up to the bike and, as I changed into my swimming gear, I received a text from Morris that he was on his way. I researched taking the back routes instead of the awful busy highway, and soon it seemed like every kid in Longreach had arrived to go swimming. Some were dropped off, some walked, some rode bicycles, and some drove. The kids jumped off the bridge or climbed a tree and hurtled into the river. Many of the kids brought floating devices and rope to hang from the tree and swing into the river. It was becoming a very busy afternoon. Unlike our last swim, this time humans would surround us.

Chapter Eight

Morris the Cowboy

While waiting for Morris to arrive, Della and I watched the children swimming in the Thompson River and jumping from trees, ropes, and the bridge; they had no adult supervision, shouting and laughing and having a great time. Luckily, no one was injured during the swimming and jumping. While I was watching the children in the river, an older man rode up on a bicycle. He parked, removed his fluro work shirt and replaced it with a regular buttoned collared shirt before opening his bicycle bag and extracting a beer. I assumed he was the owner of the tent and bicycle trailer (this was my first time meeting with someone traveling around like me) so I excitedly introduced myself. His name was Errol but he denied being the owner or knowing who it belonged to, he informed me he came to the river every day at the same time to have a drink and enjoy the cool breeze but had never seen anyone at the tent and trailer. It was then that I decided if I didn't see the owner that night, I would talk to the police, because no-one would leave their stuff unattended, for days on end. I worried the person had gone bike riding and something had happened - probably lying injured somewhere. Errol offered me a beer, and when I declined, he said he would bring ice and a soft drink for me when he next stopped for his daily ritual. Not long after all the kids began to leave. I sat at the picnic shelter with Della lying under the table having a sleep, when cowboy hat wearing Morris pulled up in his ute. I was so glad to see him I jumped up, ran over and gave him a hug and Morris hugged me back. He'd brought a cold beer for him and a bottle of wine for me and we sat and had our cool drinks at the picnic table, updating me about the horses. Jonesy worked full-time at the feedlot and Charlie was in the nearby paddock. He explained Pat was using the packsaddle to cart supplies up the mountain to fix her fence. After a general catch up, Morris leaned over to kiss me and I eagerly responded. I needed to take a shower but found the tap water was warm, as it had been sitting in a water tower above the restrooms. I quickly finished, put Della on the leash and we walked back to Morris. He had set up his large swag on the ground between his ute and the bush. I was excited about where things would go as I had been thinking about being with Morris for quite a while.

Morris left the swag early the next morning and when I finally awoke, the two local wild roosters were hanging around the swag. I let Della off the leash to play chase then carried hot water and cups to the picnic table where Morris was sitting, playing on his computer. I made us hot drinks, and after telling him about my dreadful experiences with the bicycle and road trains, I made the decision it would be safer and less trouble to hitchhike the rest of the way to Dampier. While we were talking, a local council worker arrived and I went to speak to him about the tent and bicycle trailer. He informed me the stuff belonged to the local vagrant, kicked out of the city park by police. He'd relocated to this camping area. The worker told me to stay away if he should return, as he'd probably be intoxicated and violent. Morris and I decided to head into town to visit the Australian Stockman's Hall of Fame. He helped me load my bike and supplies into the back of his ute. It took quite a while to sort out the supplies, having to downsize again, traveling with my swag and only two bags - one of food and our medical supplies and the other bag clothes, toiletries, sleeping bag, and pillow. When we arrived in town, we stopped at the bakery where Morris bought takeaway breakfast and we headed for the huge museum. In the car park, we put Della on the leash in front of the ute and gave her a bucket of water. Della likes to lay in the shade under vehicles, so that's where she went to have a sleep. We walked towards the museum and I took snapshots outside the building, before heading inside. The Stockman's Hall of Fame was definitely worth the visit. I enjoyed reading the history of the drovers, stock routes, and rodeo winners. The pictures, videos and movies were informative and interesting. The museum had a man-cage on display and I jokingly told Morris that I was going to put him in it. This man-cage was used for trapping poachers trespassing on private property. As we walked along looking at the displays, it was fun to hold Morris' hand.

We left the museum to check on Della and top up her water then headed for the top floor of the museum to see the wonderful pictures in the Art Gallery. We left the museum, and took a stroll around the stone buildings on the property, before deciding to go back to the Longreach Waterhole for a swim. Our beer and wine had been sitting in the ute all day and everything was hot. We managed to buy a cooler bag; I filled it up with ice from the machine in the back of the store and put our drinks in it. When we arrived at the waterhole, it was deserted so we walked down the boat ramp for a swim. I suggested to Morris he leave his shirt and hat on to protect his head and shoulders from burning (I always wear my hat and shirt in the water. It keeps me from sunburn and I stay cooler when I get out of the water). In the peace of the Thompson River, we cooled down, swimming around with Della until some kids arrived. They yelled and jumped off the bridge on the other side of the river and we returned to the quiet of the picnic area. Errol showed up with a soft drink and a bag of ice for me so we all had a drink and a good chat. A few beers later, tipsy Errol wobbled off on his bicycle and I began cooking dinner. The children ended up leaving and we had the camping spot to ourselves again. Della ate her dog food and Morris and I took a shower under the water tap outside the men's restroom. After a cuddle, Morris and I drifted off to sleep lying on his swag under the stars.

Morris and I woke early but I felt anxious - worried and excited about getting a lift to arrive in Katherine in time to meet Alexandria. I'd found her on the 'Gumtree' website the previous day and she was offering a lift to Western Australia. We dressed and packed our things and Morris drove Della and I into town to the local truckers' petrol station. He bought me a hot chocolate and we stood around outside observing the road trains and vehicles arriving. We watched the direction the vehicles arrived from, if they had space for swags in the back or strapped on the roof. We saw a few readying to return to their station but they were filled with jerry cans, supplies and motorbikes. A couple of retired couples driving motor homes or hauling a camping trailer came through and I approached a road train driven by a married couple. I knew they were going the wrong way, but asked if they could get on the radio to check if any trucks were going in my direction. When I found his radio only had a three-kilometer range, we agreed it wouldn't be much use. I approached another man filling his ute with petrol but he said he was heading to Emerald. I looked around a while longer and soon Morris hinted he had to head home and, eventually he couldn't delay any longer. He gave me a hug and kiss goodbye. As he was going, I approached a shaggy, blond, surfer-looking, middle-aged bloke cleaning out his old empty ute and asked him where he was headed and he said Darwin. I asked if we could have a lift to Darwin and he said, "yes, but aren't you with him", pointing to Morris's blue ute exiting the petrol station. I quickly explained Morris was going to Oakey, and Della and I were headed for Western Australia. I suggested that Katherine, in the Northern Territory would be an ideal drop off spot for us as I had found Alexandria on the internet website – 'Gumtree'. She was passing through Katherine and had agreed to give us a lift. In his rearview mirror, Morris saw what was happening, pulled over and parked, and walked to us and helped to load my stuff and tie it down in the back of the ute. The blokes had a bit of a chat and I hugged Morris goodbye again. I was feeling so excited about the start of a new adventure that I forgot to feel sad saying goodbye to Morris.

We climbed into the old white ute and Della sat on the floor as I briefly described Della and my trip across Australia. The Youngy explained that he had flown to

Brisbane and caught a train to Ipswich to buy this ute and drive it home to Darwin. He had found the ute for sale on the Internet and it reminded him of one his dad used to drive when he was young, so he wanted it. The ute was in good condition despite being old, but it had no radio or air conditioning. It soon became sweltering even with both of the front windows rolled down and the floor air vents open. First Della laid on the floor of the ute, then she stood up and placed her front paws on me, hanging her head out the window to cool down. It was stifling especially with Della half sitting on my lap. Every time we stopped to top-up the fuel, we climbed out too so I could give Della water and refill my water bottles. In Winton, we halt briefly at a tiny Retrovision shop so we could buy an iPod attachment. We plugged it into his cigarette lighter, attached his iPod to it and played music through the speakers. Out of the two days travel in the ute with Youngy, I only recognized four songs. He liked listening to instrumental aboriginal-sounding music with guitars – I have no idea what this type of music is called. It was hard to talk with both windows down because of the noisy air-tunnel it created. He did manage to tell me a story of how he sea-kayaked around the northern part of Western Australia with a mate. (It sounded quite an adventure, kayaking the Kimberly's with waterfalls pouring off the cliffs.) We saw live dingoes on the sides of the road on both of those days. The dingoes would stand still and stare at us, than walk back into the bush as we flashed by. Della and I hadn't traveled this fast the whole adventure. As Morris would say, Youngy 'can cover ground'.

Drinking hot water was horrible and not refreshing at all, but I didn't have enough money to buy cold water from a petrol station. I would get Della water at every stop we made. The water from the faucets came out hot, even if it was labelled 'cold'. It was hard on us, with the temperature over 40 Celsius and we stopped in Mount Isa so Youngy could get mobile reception to transfer money to pay for the ute he was driving. I found that quite strange, that the seller would allow Youngy (who was a stranger he'd just met on the internet) to drive away in the ute without paying for it. The seller trusted Youngy to transfer the money to his account when the banks were open. Youngy said he offered to stay in Ipswich but the owner said it was okay if he took the ute and transferred the money on Monday. I was very surprised that someone would be so trusting. I did a lot of thinking and wondering about that whole situation, but I didn't voice any of my opinions or concerns. Since there wasn't much to do in the ute, I could do a lot of thinking. Mount Isa had a slightly cooler breeze and cloud cover, so I tied Della in the back of the ute, during our stop. Della liked that a lot more than being stuck in the cramped hot ute. Around 11pm, we ended up at a rest stop just before Three Ways Roadhouse. Youngy slept in the back of his ute in his swag and I slept on the ground on top of my swag with Della sleeping next to me. The temperature didn't change much at all. It was a very hot, dry night but Youngy was up at daybreak and we started back on the road again. During the day, when I had mobile reception, I would text Alexandria to let her know the time we would be arriving in Katherine. She texted back that she would be in Katherine around 10am, on the day we were arriving. The next morning, Youngy pulled off into a rubbish tip and we found a board to make a shelter for Della in the back of the ute.

Della in back of Youngy's ute

Now able to lay under the board in the shade, Della had a breeze back there, more room to move, and lots more to look at. I silently wished I could sit in the back with her - it would have been comfortable and breezier. At 3pm, on the second day of traveling, Della and I were dropped off at Katherine Visitors' Information Centre. I waited under a shady tree on the grass with her, texting Alexandria. I tried calling but her phone was out of service. Fearing she'd already left Katherine, I accessed the 'Gumtree' website and re-read Roland's advert. Roland had already called me twice about a lift to Broome but he sounded like he wanted money up-front for the lift. His photo on 'Gumtree' showed a really cute young German and I didn't particularly want to travel with a 'hot' bloke. I felt desperate and didn't know what else to do, so I gave Roland a call. I explained I couldn't contact Alexandria and thought she'd already left Katherine and we had nowhere to go. He seemed happy to hear from me, but disappointed that he was second choice of traveling companion. Roland explained his situation to me - he was staying in Katherine at a hostel - ready to leave, he didn't want to travel to Western Australia on his own. He was in the middle of fixing a crack in his windshield of his four-wheel drive wagon and, as soon as he'd finished, he'd pick us up.

It was a very hot day, I was in sore need of a shower, and I knew Della wanted to swim. We had a quick look around for a river or some water to soak in, but there was none to be found. So, on the grass under the shady tree in front of the Katherine Visitors Information Centre, with our two bags and swag wondering when we would come across some cool refreshing water, Della and I waited for Roland.

Chapter Nine
Cozy Roland

With Della next to me, I was sitting on the swag daydreaming when I looked up and there was Roland standing in front of us. He looked better than his Internet picture. I was bedazzled by his looks – *this man is beautiful* I thought, as I jumped up, gave him a hug and thanked him for coming to our rescue. He helped me load our supplies in his red landcruiser, declared he'd be ready to leave Katherine the next day and asked where I would be staying that night. He explained he was living in a hostel and couldn't have Della and me there. I replied I had no idea - I would just camp somewhere. He dropped us off at the Katherine Springs for a swim. Della and I hadn't had a swim or a shower since Longreach - two days previous. We had done a lot of sweating and endured a lot of heat in those two days we definitely needed a bath! When we arrived, I saw the 'no dogs allowed' sign, but I put Della on the leash and we walked down the steps to the springs and nobody around us seemed to mind. Roland left with my gear in his vehicle to meet his French friend to go for a swim. I did worry a little about the gear being carted away by someone I'd met just five minutes ago, but at that moment, a swim was foremost in my mind and far more appealing than worrying about someone taking off with my used and battered supplies. I tied Della up until the other people swimming had left the water then Della and I plunged in. Some backpackers showed up, but they thought it was cute to see Della swimming so I let her stay in the water. I was relieved to see Roland and the French guy show up but they went for a swim in a nearby pool and by this time, I was waterlogged and wrinkly from being in the water so long. Della and I climbed out and walked to the other pool to see the guys. Roland was swimming in the pool, but when he saw us, he climbed up the embankment to talk. I stood looking down into his gorgeous blue eyes listening to him speak English, with his German accent, and knew Roland was the most gorgeous man I'd seen in a long time. Tall, muscular and handsome. He spoke about the trip to Broome but I can't say that I was listening. I was too busy looking at this glorious man to focus on what he was saying. I wondered how it would be travelling with him. Roland gave me his keys and I walked to the car, made myself a hot drink and waited for him and his French mate. When they returned from their swim, we drove to Woolies. Roland wanted to pick up some supplies for the trip and Della needed some dog food, so the French guy walked back to the hostel from the Woolies car park and I waited while Roland went to the bottle shop. We were parked in front of the police station and it was a very busy scene. There were a number of Aboriginal people yelling, fighting, swearing, and just causing a ruckus. It was quite entertaining as Della and I watched all the action from the car window. Roland returned with his grog to the car, and we went into Woolies. I quickly bought Della's food and returned to her in the car to observe all the action outside. The drunken Aboriginals were still creating quite a loud scene when Roland returned with his purchases and we left.

At his hostel I helped him clean and sort out his vehicle for the trip and he thought Della and I should sleep the night in his car. He had built a proper bed in the back of his landcruiser. He'd fixed up the inside of his vehicle with neon lights along the roof, speakers, curtains, and psychedelic wallpaper on the ceiling. So Roland went into the hostel, I slept in the 'party car' and Della napped on the ground under it. As night fell, the temperature didn't cool down until well after midnight - it was a very hot night. I slept with all the windows opened and, as usual, woke early. I didn't seem to be able to sleep past 5am. I sorted out my things and waited for Roland. I looked around and saw this was yet another vehicle with no air conditioning. I sighed, thinking why can't we ever get a hitch with air-con? As arranged Roland showed up promptly at 7 and we loaded his gear, filled the water jerrys and headed off. Our first stop was the petrol station, we filled up the tank and the petrol can. Roland told me his USB stick had over 5,000 songs on it that sounded promising until he told me it contained jazz piano music and the Beatles.

Along the road, we stopped off at a river and Della ran down the steep embankment for a swim. Wearing our thongs, Roland and I made our way downhill after her. This was something we regretted later. Looking out for crocodiles, we swam in the shallow river and thankfully, we didn't see any. I didn't really want to wrestle a crocodile if it went for Della. I didn't need that much adventure. Although the water was warm, we felt refreshed after the swim but it was hard work trying to walk back up the steep embankment in wet thongs. My feet kept sliding backwards and I gave up halfway and removed the thongs. We finally arrived at the border of Northern Territory and Western Australia and there was a man working at the quarantine gate. We stopped, the officer showed me a clipboard of prohibited items and I acknowledged I had nuts, so he wanted to look through the vehicle. I showed him my bag of roasted cashews and he said that was fine. Then he started looking through Roland's things and found two bags of carrots and a bag of tomatoes. He commented sarcastically 'so you don't shop together?' (I think he was upset we hadn't declared the vegetables but they weren't mine and I wasn't going to declare them for Roland. I figured Roland could do that for himself. I think the officer thought that I knew those things were in the vehicle and I didn't mention them on purpose.) This was my first day traveling with Roland and we hadn't shopped together but if I had explained that to the officer, he would think I was lying and made up the excuse. So I just left the matter, by keeping my mouth shut and letting him search the vehicle. The officer gave us a lecture and talked about fines but allowed us to drive away.

I felt a little irritated but soon forgot about it as we saw our turnoff for Lake Argyle. We turned down a very long road to the beautiful lake and drove around looking for a camping spot, but there was none to be found, 'No camping' signs were everywhere. The only camping at the Lake was at the official campground but we were on a tight budget, and didn't want to splurge on a paid campsite. After taking pictures at lookouts and looking for a place to camp we decided to enquire the price.

The guy at the counter was friendly and said it was $14 per night, per person and Della was $20, although her fee was refundable the next day as long as she obeyed the rules and we had no loud parties. I assured the campground manager that I would explain the rules to Della. She never has loud parties, as she doesn't really like socialising with other dogs. Della just likes to hang out with me. We decided to stay the night. It was a good decision the infinity swimming pool looked fantastic and we jumped into it straight away. The water was clear and cool and we felt refreshed. I was able to take my first proper shower since Isisford, Queensland. I ended up taking three showers in total and we only spent one night there! The camp kitchen had a refrigerator and we put that to good use with our drinks and water. Roland had brought his fishing rods and we walked down the side of the mountain to a fishing spot with his foldable camp chairs and fishing gear. I threw out the lure three times but it kept tangling in the seaweed, so I lost interest in fishing straight away. Roland kept saying fishing required patience, so I told him he could do the fishing and I would gaze at the gorgeous views. It was lovely to relax and watch him whilst weaving all sorts of romantic situations with Roland in my head. The rest of the scenery was also delightful we were in a gorge with large colourful rocks on all sides, a few lonely trees growing on top of the mountains and a few boats in the blue water of the huge lake. Unfortunately the fish didn't bite and when we climbed our way back up that mountain. We were all hot and sweaty again and jumped into the pool to cool off. After our swim, I washed our laundry in the sink and hung it on the line to dry. In the camp kitchen, Roland made pasta and sauce and I made apple pie for dessert. We both had a few drinks and Roland ended up getting very drunk. We had a chat to a couple that had been traveling around Western Australia for eighteen months (that's a long time to be traveling in one state but Western Australia is enormous and there are a lot of places to visit). They were on their way to Northern Territory to explore there.

In the morning, when I woke, Roland was lying next to the swag on the mattress. He said it was too hot to sleep in the car, so he'd pulled out the mattress from the back of the car and slept outdoors in the cool nighttime breeze. We had porridge for breakfast, a swim, and a shower before packing. We drove to the boat ramp and Roland did some fishing off the jetty. He caught a catfish, but he put it back into the water as he didn't like to eat catfish. I felt so hot I went for a swim and Della came too but there was a large amount of seaweed in the water. Now on his own, Roland soon became bored with fishing and decided to come for a swim. I looked into an abandoned boat, parked on the jetty, and saw some noodles (floatation devices). I climbed into the boat and borrowed two for us to use in the water. We didn't have to worry about the seaweed and could sit on our noodles in the water and I taught Della how to float on a noodle. It was a lot more fun swimming with the noodles.

A man came down, filled up the engine motors and vacuumed the abandoned boat parked on the jetty. As he was leaving he asked if those were his noodles we were using and Roland nodded. He became really angry, told us we had trespassed on his boat and he was going to call the police to report us. He wrote down Roland's vehicle plate number and told us to leave the noodles on the jetty. We tried to explain that we had just borrowed them but he wouldn't listen and said he would get the Police to search our car to find drugs or find something wrong with the car so it wasn't roadworthy and arrest us for it.

Then he stormed off. I became quite worried, as I knew Roland's car wouldn't pass a roadworthy test. I didn't want to have his car impounded. Della and I would have to find another lift. Roland was more upset about the drugs comment. I didn't understand why, until he mentioned that he had marijuana in the car. I was shocked and straight began into panic.

I told Roland 'I hope you hid your pot better than you hid your carrots and tomatoes.'

He said he didn't hide the pot at all. I replied that we had better hide it quick so the cops wouldn't find it. Alarmed, all I could think of was what if they have sniffer dogs? We are so screwed. I'll be going to jail and I haven't even smoked a cigarette, let alone done drugs…EVER!

So Roland found his pot and it wasn't much at all, wouldn't even have made a whole cigarette, but I didn't want to risk it. He suggested smoking it then we wouldn't have to worry. I didn't vote for that idea and replied' I don't smoke and you don't want the police to pull us over and find you're stoned'. By now I was frantic and we had a hysterical conversation about where to hide it. After various suggestions I figured Della would be a good place. The police would search the car and us, but not Della. If they had sniffer dogs, their dogs might bark at Della, but the police would assume it's because she's a dog. So we took the small amount of pot in its plastic bag, attaching it with black electrical tape, to the inside of Della's collar so that it wasn't noticeable. Della has fluffy fur around her neck anyways and her collar is barely seen. So we returned the noodles to the jetty, drove to the campground and picked up our drinks from the freezer.

On the drive to Kununurra, we practiced our story. We needed to get our story straight. I acted like I was the cop pulling Roland over and asking questions. First we decided on the almost truth, but with Roland climbing into the boat for the noodles. Then we decided he just reached over the side of the boat and grabbed the noodles, so his body wasn't trespassing, only his arm. Unfortunately, I soon found that Roland was terrible at answering my 'policeman' questions. I'd ask a question and he would say in his broken English, 'I don't have drugs officer.' I would reply between clenched teeth 'I didn't even ask you if you had drugs, I asked if you stepped onto the boat.' He was a disaster. I wailed that he didn't answer correctly we'd definitely get searched.' You can't bring up drugs, when the cops haven't even asked the question yet. It will make you look guilty.' After a while I calmed down and decided the best story would be deny, deny, deny. So we practiced the 'deny' story and Roland coped better with that version. I told him to say two things 'I did not go for boat ride' in very broken English and to say 'I do not understand, please speak slowly.' I told Roland he would do all the talking and I would just act like I don't talk at all and pray they don't ask to check my identity. We entered Kununurra, and the first stop was the Visitors Centre, to get a map and information about the area. We left there and Roland went shopping in Woolies whilst Della and I hung out on the grass under the tree. We stopped and bought petrol before we left town, and no police stopped us. The cops must have been busy with more important matters, than the borrowing of noodles from a boat and I heaved a sigh of relief.

Our next stop was a rest area in Spring Creek and we set up camp. The creek had just enough water to cool down and rinse us off. Della, of course, loved it and went swimming. I looked for crocodiles but soon saw the creek wasn't big enough to hold any. We had dinner. Roland wanted a cozy fire in the fire-pit, so I helped him collect wood. We had drinks, listened to my music on my IPAD and watched the fire burn itself to ash. I slept in the swag and Roland slept in the back of his car. In the morning, we packed the land cruiser and headed to the highway, and took 'hitching naked' pictures along the highway with Della. Roland took pictures of me nude, walking along the side of the highway with Della, and then I took pictures of him walking along nude with Della. I had suggested to Roland that we do this the night before whilst having drinks around the fire. After our photos shoot, we drove into Hall's Creek and stopped at the Visitors Centre. A very lovely bloke gave us a map and told us about the Sawpit Gorge and we decided to go for a drive and visit it. Driving along we stopped at the China Wall and took snaps then headed to Caroline Pool and had a lovely swim, until the fish started biting me and I jumped out. The next stop was the Old Post Office ruins and the town cemetery. We walked around, reading the headstones that I found it very interesting. Most headstones listed how the person died – one showed the man died of thirst. I empathized it went through my mind that could easily have happened to me on this trip.

We continued down the red dirt road to Palm Springs, a waterhole full of laughing Aboriginal children. The kids liked to climb to up high and jump off into the water. We went for a swim as well and the kids seemed to like Della and they climbed all over me as I was sitting on a submerged rock. Heading off to the final destination of Sawpit Gorge, we did some four wheel driving across the creek and parked. By now I knew that Roland loved the word 'cozy,' and he wanted to find a cozy camping spot.

He says cozy so much, that I wished I had a Thesaurus so I could find another similar word for Roland to use.

We started walking towards the gorge to take photos, when Roland slipped in his thongs and almost tore off the nail on his big toe. One look at his bleeding toe and I had him limping back to the car. I pulled out my medical supply kit and began cleaning and bandaging him up. He didn't seem to mind the pain after I had him swallow two prescription painkillers. When I finished working, his toe had a huge bandage on it. Whilst Roland elevated his foot and relaxed Della and I went for a swim but we didn't like the water as it was very hot and full of seaweed. We returned to Roland and suggested we camp by Palm Springs as that waterhole was much nicer. I drove through the creek, up the embankment with the four wheel drive on, and we arrived back at Palm Springs.

There were three utes parked and the waterhole was full of local Aboriginals drinking. They had loud music playing from their utes. I didn't mind the music because I was so sick of Roland's Beatles and piano jazz music. Roland didn't like their country and rock music and when a group of them wanted to leave and their ute wouldn't start, Roland tried to help. He used jumper cables but that didn't work, so they asked for a push-start. Roland didn't know what that was, so I tried explaining it to him but he seemed to think that we were going to crash into their ute. So I took over and told him I would do the driving. I showed him how to push start a vehicle, the first few goes didn't work, so I was about ready to call it a day, when one of the guys noticed the immobiliser was on. He switched that off and the next push we gave turned his motor over and he was ready to go. We said goodbye as they all piled into his ute and took off for town. Della and I went for a swim, and then collected wood for a fire and it began raining so the three of us sat in the land cruiser. The rain scared off the rest of the group, they all piled into the remaining utes and headed for town. Peace returned and we had the whole area to ourselves. After the rain, we started up the fire and I set up my swag. Roland wanted to have a bath, so we got our shower supplies and headed for the pool. Roland tied a plastic bag over his left foot to keep it dry while he took a bath. He then slid backwards into the water off a rock, still keeping his damaged foot on top of the rock. He was in a very shallow area and not fully submerged. I climbed into the pool behind him and helped pick him up and move him to the far side of the rock were the water was deeper. He still managed to keep his foot on the rock and not get it wet. I then handed him his bath products, as he needed them, while I took my bath. I was puzzled that Roland hadn't made any moves towards me despite the running around naked, baths, swims, changing clothes in front of each other. After we were done washing, I helped him back up towards the dry area of the rock and we walked back to the campsite, had our meal, a chat, and then went to sleep. Roland had two tents, but liked to sleep in the back of the land cruiser. I slept in my swag, as usual.

In the morning, we packed up and headed back to Hall's Creek and on to Fitzroy Crossing. We stopped off at the rest area at Mary Pool on the way and drove over the Mary River Bridge. It was an old bridge, the water on one side was high and went right up to the edge and I noticed there were holes in the base of the brick part of the bridge, where water poured through the holes into the pool on the other side. We drove around the rest area looking for a 'cozy' (Roland's word again) spot for camping. We parked and walked along the river, but, without sinking into the mud, there was no easy access to the river. The only access to the pool was by the bridge, so we jumped back into the land cruiser and found a spot near the bridge. We made a firepit lined with stones and we took a walk around, gathering branches and wood. The wood was very solid and heavy and we didn't need much to make a fire to last all night. I went for a swim with Della while Roland walked down the river to find a fishing spot and when we returned, we found Roland fishing on the far side of the river. He hadn't caught anything and eventually came back disappointed and lay down on a blanket under the shady tree. We were both feeling the heat and Roland wanted to go for a dip so we walked down to the bridge and, after he placed his foot in the plastic bag and tied it shut, I helped him into the pool. He lay in the pool with his hurt plastic wrapped foot on the rock whilst Della and I went for a swim.

One of the holes in the bridge brick-work had a steady stream of water rushing through it was fun to try to swim against the current. We watched a lizard living in one of the bridge holes for a while it poked its head out into the sunshine and if one of us moved it would withdraw into its lair. We tried to stay still but it was hard because we were too near the current. After a while I became bored watching the scared lizard, and my gaze fell on handsome Roland floating on his back with his foot propped up on the rock. I swam up behind him and playfully surprised him by putting my arms around his chest. Roland leaned back and slowly turned his head round to look at me. Our attraction was too great I leaned forward and kissed him. Roland responded kissing me back. I enjoyed Roland's kisses but began to feel uncomfortable because I had been in Morris's arms only the week before. Starting to feel guilty, I stopped kissing him and told Roland I was getting out of the water. He wanted to stay so Della and I climbed out of the pool and walked back up to our campsite. Some time later, Roland returned and lay down on the blanket next to me and we had begun kissing again when a car pulled up next to our campsite and parked. It looked like they were going to stay the night. We looked at one another and shrugged. We would have preferred the whole rest area to ourselves but yet another vehicle turned up so Della and I went for a swim to cool off.

On our return, some cows were wandering around the campsite, so I decided to teach Della to round up the cows, but Della just wasn't at all interested, all she wanted to do was chase sticks. Della wasn't paying attention, especially since these cows turned to stare her down when she approached. The cows gave Della the 'evil eye' and she turned around and ran back to me. I told Della that she would be fired from a cattle station the first day at work and ended up running around the campground chasing cows with Della following me and not learning anything. Della didn't care; she didn't want to roundup the stubborn cows that knew we were invading their grazing area. We walked back to the campsite and Roland and I went swimming in the pool. He didn't care about getting his sore toe wet anymore.

A local Aboriginal woman, with her little girl, came along and we had a chat about the bridge and pool. She said that during the wet season, the bridge usually went under water. She left and Roland climbed all the way to the bridge against the current coming from the hole under the bridge. When we walked back to the campsite, I tried to get the fire going before it started to rain. I didn't succeed because the wind was too strong so I placed some flat bark around the dry leaves so they stayed dry whilst we waited in the car, hoping the rain would stop. The shower didn't last long and we soon had the fire going for the night. Roland erected the 4-person blue tent and he put the foam mattress and blankets in the tent. The rain had cooled things off slightly but it was still muggy but we had the place to ourselves again as the other vehicles left during the rain. Roland said it was 'cozy' he just loved the word 'cozy' and managed to use it in almost every sentence. After our meal we decided to go for a swim in the pool. We were completely on our own, nothing moved for miles around and our clothes felt heavy so we took them off. We walked all the way to the bridge in the nude and went for a swim. It was dark out and I was worried about water snakes, so we didn't stay in the water long. The water was vert warm too and wasn't cooling me down, but it was good just to rinse off.

With the help of my solar-powered flashlight, which I shone behind me so Roland could see where he was stepping, we walked back. I was concerned about his damaged toe and didn't want him to stub it again. We all went to sleep in the tent together and woke up in the morning to heavy rain. When I climbed out of the tent I found the cold rain was coming down hard enough to have a shower but I refrained from getting out the soap. It didn't look like it was going to clear up anytime soon so, still naked, we started to pack up camp. It was pretty useless getting dressed, as our clothes would have quickly become sodden in the heavy downpour.

In the distance, some cars tried to cross the flooded bridge but the drivers decided against it. I put a shirt on and wrapped a towel around my waist and Roland drove us slowly towards the bridge, now under water. I was concerned about the strong current and told him that I would walk over the bridge first and he should wait in the car. I figured if I got swept into the water I could swim, but the car couldn't. So wearing Heidi's purple shirt and a blue towel around my waist, I set out to walk through the water. The current was very strong at some points and almost swept me off my feet. My shirt and towel were tugged around by the wind and rain but I managed to keep my balance. On the other side of the bridge there was a white work-van waiting. The bloke climbed out and asked about the current and I replied that it was strong and I thought it safer to wait till the rain stopped and the water went down. Just then, as we were talking, behind me I heard an engine. It was Roland in the land cruiser. He had driven up right behind me!! I was stunned and yelled over the noise of the rain that it wasn't safe, and not to move but he shrugged and told me not to worry. I couldn't walk fast enough to get out of his way to the other side of the narrow bridge and was stopping him from crossing. There he was, just sitting on the bridge in his vehicle with water gushing around the car. I was petrified, my baby, Della, was in the car too what if the vehicle got swept away and Della was stuck in the car? She couldn't roll down the window or open the door to escape she'd drown. I grabbed hold of the front of the land cruiser as it came near and pulled myself round to the passenger door. If the car was swept away, with Della in it, I wanted to be there to help her to safety. I didn't give Roland and his damaged foot a second's thought if he was stupid enough to drive over a flooded bridge without checking, he was second on my 'save' list. Della would have waited until I told her it was okay to cross the bridge, but Della didn't have that choice.

The guy quickly climbed back in his work-van and reversed it out of the roadway so Roland could drive through. I snapped 'you might as well go the rest of the way across the bridge now and hurry up'. At any moment, a large tree trunk could float down in that swirling current, and sweep us right off the bridge. I held my breath, my mind a whirl of dangerous situations but we made it safely across. We stopped to talk to the bloke in the van. He had a two-wheel drive and he said he'd decided not to cross the bridge. Relieved we were out of danger, I told him that was a smart decision, as I wouldn't have crossed the bridge had I been driving even in the four- wheel drive. Someone who had no knowledge of what river currents can do took that decision out of my hands. We said goodbye to the man and started driving west towards Fitzroy Crossing. On the way, I explained to Roland the source of my fear concerning the flooded bridge that every year in Australia people die in floods and storm water drains by doing the same mindless thing he had just done.

Chapter Ten

Covering Ground

After our dicey bridge adventure, we stopped at the Fitzroy Crossing Visitors Centre to ask about the condition of the Gibb River Road and the Windjana Gorge National Park. We were informed that both of them were closed to tourists due to the wet season. The lady was helpful and suggested the open Gelkie Gorge National Park that was nearby.

We drove to the Gelkie Gorge and I changed into jeans and the Centre staff recommended hiking boots too. We headed down the trail with Della in the lead. Roland wanted to walk slowly because of his injured foot and Della wanted to run. So I told Roland that we'd run ahead and wait for him under a shady tree as it was heating up. I think Roland was a bit grumpy about that idea, but I wanted to run as much as Della as we'd been cooped up in the vehicle all day. We stopped along the way and took some pictures and read signs warnings about people who'd died from climbing the unstable limestone rock.

Returning to Roland's land cruiser, Della jumped into the back of the vehicle just as a park ranger pulled up in a yellow sports car. The ranger was a large aboriginal

Hiking Gelkie Gorge National Park

lady, wearing a blue shirt and she gave us a lecture about Della being in the park and the fines we could incur. I apologised and said I didn't realise that Della couldn't be in the park and that we were leaving. She said we would have to leave 'right now' stating there were clear 'no dogs allowed' signs at the entrance of the park. I was in the middle of changing out of my jeans and assured her that we were leaving. The park ranger climbed into her car and drove off as I finished changing into shorts. In the car Roland insisted on rolling a cigarette and having a smoke before we left but I felt sure the ranger would be back and I was right. Her car pulled up and she very abruptly told us we'd had enough time to leave. Roland hadn't even lit his cigarette, but he grumbled and started the car and we followed the ranger's yellow sports car to the park entrance she was determined to see the back of us.

We returned to Fitzroy Crossing to do some shopping at the local supermarket and Roland looked for bait at the fishing/camping store. We filled up at the petrol station and took a shower in the rest rooms before heading to Telegraph Pool. It was getting late so we decided to stop for the night at the Boab Rest area where there was an amazing large hollow-trunk tree in the middle of the park. We could hear frogs croaking and the center of the tree smelled odd. I lifted Della and put her in the middle but she didn't want to sniff around and just jumped out. While I cooked dinner, Roland erected the tent under the tree and collected wood, starting a fire in the fire pit. Before going to sleep, I put Della on the lead because we were so close to the highway – I worried about her wandering onto the road in the middle of the night. The next morning Roland offered muesli for breakfast and I declined but he brought out my favorite cereal and I changed my mind. I found Roland called all breakfast cereals, 'muesli'. I tried to explain that breakfast cereals can be quite different, but hesitated and decided observing the packet would be my first priority next time Roland offered to share food. I wasn't impressed with Roland's food supply, he didn't close the bags properly and ants found their way in. I pointed out the ants and Roland said it just added protein before properly closing the bag, ants and all. As long as his items were unopened, his pasta, rice, or tinned baked beans were fine to eat but eating Roland's food required a lot of observation before agreeing to share and I stuck to my food as much as possible. We packed up camp and headed to Willare Bridge Roadhouse where we stopped and took showers. Following directions from the cook we headed down a long red- dirt road and parked under a tree and I found some of Della's beef jerky for Roland to use as bait for fishing. While Roland fished (but didn't get a bite) Della and I rested under a tree. We continued on further down the road and I spotted the Telegraph Pole off to the right where the bay was much bigger. Three locals were fishing from a boat and we asked if they had caught anything that morning but it seemed they were unlucky too. We found a nice 'cozy' fishing spot and Roland went to get his fishing rods only to realised he'd left his favorite one at the previous spot. We quickly tried to replace our tracks but took a wrong turn and discovered two rusted cars and an old rusty bus, which Roland stopped to photograph. We retraced our tracks, found the missing fishing rod and headed back to our 'cozy' spot. Again Roland had no luck with the fish but he did manage to entice a turtle to follow our beef jerky all the way to the shoreline. The turtle took one look at us, turned around and quickly swam away.

Della and I went for a quick dip and the local fishermen warned us they had spotted two large crocodiles in the water that morning. We climbed out of the water quicker than we climbed in! Since swimming was out of the question, I dipped our shirts in the water and we wore them wet to stay cool. We packed up the fishing gear and bumped along the four-wheel drive track that wound its way through a cattle station to the Indian Ocean. Arriving at the shoreline was a disappointment. It was extremely muddy and too shallow for fishing. Della and I had a quick dip to cool off and we took a few pictures before turning round and heading back down the incredibly bumpy track to the main road. By the time we reached the highway, I had an upset stomach and I didn't want to go four wheeling driving ever again. I was surprised Della hadn't been car sick, as she usually was when the car jerked around. We had decided to camp that night on the beach at Willie Creek Rest Area, thirty-five kilometers north of Broome. We used the GPS, which was a mistake we should have just followed the road signs. The GPS showed we had passed Willie Creek Road, so we turned around and drove down this dubious overgrown track, which had us turning around after two kilometers. Back on the main dirt road, we passed another dodgy dirt track that the GPS told us was Willie Creek Road but we ignored it in the hope there would eventually be a sign for a 'proper' dirt road. Finally we came across a sign for Willie Creek Oyster Farm and Campground. Taking that dirt road, we drove for about five kilometers following the red markers on the roadside. When we arrived at the end, there was the Oyster Farm Store and the campground. We headed to the store first to get some information about the area but it was shut and there wasn't a soul in sight. I walked around and I found a working water cooler. Oh joy!! My drink bottle was filled with water which had become hot so I emptied the bottle and filled it with cold water, astonished to see the outside of the bottle quickly covered in condensation. How lovely - a water cooler in the middle of nowhere and it was full of cold water!! I went back to the car and told Roland that I found the most amazing thing ever. He said it can't be more amazing than sex and I replied 'oh yes it is'. He walked around the building and agreed. We both had a cold drink, and filled our bottles with the wonderful cool fresh water.

Heading off to the campground, we found to our dismay there was no shade or tables, but it did have a fire pit. We wandered down to the beach, passing crocodile warning signs but it was so hot and I just wanted a quick dip to cool off. I choose a shallow clear pool and had a good look around then instructed Roland to look out for crocodiles, while Della and I went for a quick swim. The water wasn't cool – it felt like a very warm salty bath and when we got out I felt like I needed to scratch all over, the salt had coated my skin. Roland jumped in next whilst I watched for crocodiles and he ended with the same feeling. We returned to the campsite and I put Della on the lead, mindful she might feel the heat and go for a midnight swim with the crocodiles. We were miles from civilisation, it was nighttime, hot and sweaty, we took our salty wet clothes off and walked around naked. While we were cooking instant noodles, two vehicles pulled out of the oyster farm and their headlights shone on us. I grabbed a towel and wrapped it around me, whilst Roland ducked behind his vehicle. We finished our meal, and I determined we really had to remove the salt or we'd be scratching all night long. I showed Roland how to have a bush bath in the moonlight on the shore of a beach. He absolutely loved it. I didn't think it was all that great, but then I'm not a bloke. I had Roland hold the collapsible bucket of fresh water in front of him. I slipped on my looffah-glove, planting a dollop of liquid bath soap on it. Then I dipped my hands in the water and rubbed my hands all over his naked body. If the suds stopped spreading I dipped my hands in the water and applied more soap to the glove and continue on with the body washing. I washed his front, and back and I didn't miss a spot. Roland just stood there holding the water, telling me this was amazing, but then again Roland thought many things were amazing. He'd been raving about the gorge we'd seen the previous day, when I took a clean chuck-wipe, dipped that into the water and squeezed all the water out of the cloth over his body. I started rinsing him off from the shoulders downwards. The clean water ran down his hot body and took the soapsuds and salt with it. After his bath was finished it was my turn. Roland was quite disappointed when he found out that all that was required of him was to continue to hold the water bucket. I kept the glove on and washed myself and that German guy didn't get bored watching me. After scrubbing the salt away, I rinsed myself with the chucks wipe and finally had Roland dump the left-overwater over my back. We dried off but stayed naked it was still too hot for clothes. We watched the fire for a while and talked about the trip and I fell asleep in my chair. Roland woke me up and said it was time for bed. We climbed into the tent and went to sleep. The sun was out and heating up the tent when we woke. After breakfast we packed the land cruiser and drove to Cable Beach, Broome looking forward to a swim in the ocean. We drove into Broome, dropped our dirty clothes in a washing machine at a local Laundromat and then found a brewery. Della was placed under a shady tree on her lead and we walked into wonderful cool air conditioning. We sat at a table and Roland ordered beer and I drank the entire contents of a free one-liter bottle of cold water, returning to collect our wet clean-smelling clothes and driving to the local beach and water park. We hung our clothes to dry around the inside of the land cruiser and I made breakfast at the picnic shelter before hanging out in the water park. A few kids were there, but they didn't seem to mind me waiting to get sprayed with cool fresh water. In fact, their mums, sitting on the picnic bench watched me enjoying myself getting wet and cooling down, decided to join me and get wet too. A grandma even put her bathers on and came in, but for some reason she didn't want to get her hair wet. Roland came over to tell me he was going to the beach for a swim. Della wasn't allowed into the water park so, in the very blue ocean, she went for a swim with Roland.

I collected the three bags that were waiting for me at the Post Office. It was hard trying to carry the heavy, slippery, plastic post-bags to the car but I was excited. I had packed them so long ago, I'd forgotten what was in them and it felt like Christmas. I had two food bags and one supply bag. After stopping to buy food, wine, beer and fill up with fuel at the petrol station, our next stop was the camping store, Roland took so long picking out his fishing lures, but I think he just wanted to luxuriate in the air conditioning. We stopped at the library and checked our Internet for free. Then we were off again on the highway heading south. I drove until it grew dark and I'd started yawning so I pulled over at the next rest area, climbed into the back of the land cruiser and went to sleep. I couldn't be bothered cooking tea and gave Roland a protein bar to eat but he made instant noodles for himself before going to sleep.

In the morning we woke to find we had a flat tire and used Roland's air- compressor to inflate it. We decided to get it fixed in Port Hedland and stopped twice at roadhouses on the way to keep it inflated. After so much open road, the roads were now so busy it felt like city driving as we neared Port Hedland. With so much mining in the area the traffic was mainly road trains and work-utes. We stopped at the Port Hedland Tourist information Centre to find it temporally moved to the Arts Gallery so I went and picked up a map. We met Roland back at his car and pointed out the train car, now a restaurant, we had passed on the way to the Art Gallery, knowing Roland would want a photo. We drove to the Beau repairs shop to have the tire fixed but the earliest they could help was the following day so we returned to the car and checked the tourist map. We found National Tires and called them and we booked- in for that afternoon. Stopping off at Recreation Reserve we had a quick dip in the ocean and the vehicle almost got stuck in the sand on our way out. A local stopped and offered assistance, but Roland put the four-wheel drive on and let air out of the tires and we managed to make it out on our own however, we had to high-tail it to petrol station to put air back in the tires, before we drove to our appointment.

When we arrived at National Tires the guy behind the counter was very friendly and interested in our travels. He asked us to place a pin with our names on our birth towns on his world map. He not only allowed us to fill up our water bottles from his cold water cooler, he didn't charge us for fixing the tire and crumpled up the bill - it was 'on the house'. Roland was so happy and we headed to the town beach for lunch and a glass of wine at the picnic shelter. Again it was very hot so after a swim, we hung out in the water, even Della swam around for a long time. We took advantage of the showers and then stopped at Woolies for supplies before we headed out of town, I was beginning to get very tired of listening to the Beatles and Roland's jazz piano music all day so every time we got near a town, I insisted on listening to the radio. *Anything is better than listening to the same music, day in and day out.* We stopped off at a rest area and we set up the tent under the large picnic shelter. It was red dirt and lots of biting ants. Darkness approached and the mozzies were a nuisance so we climbed into the tent and went to sleep.

Following breakfast the next morning, we headed to Point Samson and Honeymoon Cove. When we arrived Roland didn't like the look of the beach but I was happy. There was sand, showers, and snorkeling. I convinced Roland to take a walk around and he decided to stay. He set up a beach shelter from the sun; we had an esky full of ice and wine, and a blanket to lay on. I went snorkeling and it was amazing seeing wonderful tropical fish and lovely colourful coral. Della enjoyed swimming and chasing the seagulls and Roland enjoyed his snorkeling and drinking. It was a wonderful relaxing morning and we were able to take showers before heading into Roebourne.

We stopped at the information office that was located at the old prison and it turned out to hold a very interesting museum. Della was welcomed inside and we sat on the chairs in the air conditioning, watching a DVD about the local area before walking round the prison, looking at the shackles. I read the notices - I hadn't realised before that Aboriginals had been used as slaves and if they ran away from the station they were sent to jail and forced into hard labor. As we left, heading to Dampier, I began to feel very excited. It slowly sunk in that Della and I had almost reached our destination. I was elated that Della and I were finally at the end of our trek. We entered Dampier and the Red Dog statue was at the Welcome sign. Della wasn't impressed with the statue but she was good and did her posing for the camera and we took a large number of snaps.

Della's Destiny

Roland and Della with Red Dog

We headed towards the beach, but the first one we came too was full of workers in orange shirts so we drove down the esplanade and found another beach that turned out to be quite rocky. We went for a swim and it was heaven to cool down, and follow it by a refreshing beach shower. We moved on to the jetty where Roland tried his hand at fishing again, but as usual he caught nothing. Back on the main highway, we headed south and stopped for the night at Miaree Pool Rest Area. We slept in the back of the car with the windows down and had a lovely cool breeze. In the morning, we went for a swim then walked back to the vehicle to sort out our belongings and hit the road.

It was Saturday and we packed up and drove a long way but couldn't find a rest stop with a waterhole, ending up in Exmouth. 'No free camping' signs were everywhere and soon Roland was stressing about where to camp. We visited the Information Centre but it was already closed for the day so we stopped at the library and police station but they were shut too. We stopped at a campground and tried to get information but the only question anyone knew an answer to was the entrance fee to the national park. I did manage to get a number for Renata, a local lady who looked after dogs while people visited the park - I really didn't want to leave Della but I didn't want a fine either.

We found the boat ramp and went fishing and took showers, checking for a camp spot on the way but there were those nasty 'no camping signs' everywhere. Heading back into town we finally found a campsite. It was after hours and a friendly Gold Coast Finks biker was the night-watchman. He checked us in and it was a lovely campground with great facilities which I took advantage of putting our esky bag in the fridge and a few bottles of water in the freezer. Once again we slept in the back of the car with Della on a blanket underneath. In the morning, we headed north along the coast and checked out the shipwreck, the superb sandy beaches, and boat jetty. We hung out at one of the sandy beaches and went swimming, but the wind was blowing and made it unpleasant. We stopped at the Turtle Centre and read up on turtles, then took showers at the boat ramp before setting off into town to drop Della at Renata's house.

Renata was a very friendly lady who seemed very nice and quite capable of caring for Della but I worried Della might escape and come looking for me with no idea where to look. Renata had a large friendly, white boxer-dog but Della was sticking close to me as she could sense my unhappiness. Despite my worries, we left Della and headed to the National Park but I called Renata to check in on Della. Apparently Della was doing fine just some whining, and she hadn't tried to jump the fence. Renata told me to stop worrying and have a good time.

We arrived at the park entrance to find the ranger station closed so we filled out the form and deposited our money in the honesty box. We were the only people at the campground but I was very depressed about leaving Della behind. I decided in future *If she can't go, then I won't go either*.

In the morning, Roland went to observe the dolphins at the beach and I took pictures of the local kangaroos. We headed to Turquoise Bay and did some snorkelling. The fish and coral were lovely there but at Lakeside it was all dead coral and not many fish. I much preferred the first spot. We visited the lighthouse and took a few pictures and Roland started drinking the cask wine becoming quite drunk. I dropped him at the fishing boat ramp, took a shower and drove into town to put air in the tires and pick up Della. She seemed fine and excited to see me. Whilst I observed Della, Renata regaled me with details of Della's day of beach, wash, bones, etc. She lay on the blanket they had given her to sleep on and seemed quite comfortable there. She wasn't scared and she looked like she wouldn't mind staying longer. I started walking towards the gate then turned around and asked Della if she coming with me and she decided to come.

Whilst Della sat in the front seat, at the petrol station I filled the tires with air and we headed back to collect Roland from the boat ramp. He'd been trying to spear fish while drunk, so I wasn't surprised when he didn't have any; I was more surprised that he hadn't speared himself. I drove out of town heading south and pulled into a 'stopping bay'. We slept in the back of the car and Della slept underneath the car on a blanket, but I kept her on the lead because we were close to the road and I didn't want her to wander and get hit by a passing car. At daylight we departed again for Coral Bay and stopped at the local supermarket, which was very small and had outrageously priced goods. Roland paid over a dollar

Roland and Della enjoying the view

for two carrots and I paid six dollars for two cans of dog food for Della. Parked at the beach, we watched a tourist boat filled with sightseers, leave from the bay as we had breakfast under a sun-shelter. It was a pleasant beach but the wind made it too cold for me to go snorkelling. Della had a swim and chased the seagulls while Roland went into the water. He eventually came ashore and lay on the blanket for a while to warm up. There were noisy people on the boat jetty and the tourist boats weren't too far away so Roland suggested finding a more remote spot. We had been spoiled having had so many beaches to our-selves, so we packed up, got in the car and headed down another four-wheel drive track and found a great spot on top of a hill overlooking the ocean.

When we set off again, this time to the Blowholes seventy kilometers north of Carnarvon, we passed the large 'King Waves Kill' sign and pulled into a camping spot which turned out to be a shanty town. The sign told us it cost $5.50 a night and to report to the ranger before camping. We drove around looking for the ranger and the place looked very strange. There were little shacks - some made of wood, others of rusty steel and tin and lots of little outhouses, some with water tanks on top. The little shacks had numbers on them reminding me of the favelas in Rio de Janeiro, Brazil. We drove slowly and came upon an orange bus with a satellite dish out-front. Roland wanted to take a picture and as he approached the bus, a woman came out and said she was living there, she was a tourist too and camping was free. Roland took his picture and came back to the car and we drove around looking for a spot to camp and came upon a 'Ranger' sign and stopped. Holding a beer, a long-haired surfer came out of the hut and started talking to us. Meanwhile another guy left the shack and walked towards an outhouse and peed outside, on the scrub. The 'ranger' said we could just camp anywhere. I mentioned that the shacks and outhouses had padlocks on them so they must belong to someone. His reply was the locals owned the shacks, but only there at Christmas, Easter, and fishing time. The property belonged to the government and no-one owned the land so it was fine to camp there. He said we would need a chemo toilet, which we didn't have, so he said we could use his. The surfer and his mates looked like a rough crew and I didn't want to be wandering over there to use their toilet in the middle of the night. We decided shack 34 would be our home. It was blue, with a nice carpet-covered verandah and shade sails on two sides. There was also a large fire-pit in front and an old flat Barbie we could use as a kitchen table. Roland erected the tent on the covered verandah. The doors entering the shack were padlocked so we didn't get to have a look inside. We found some old wood in a pile outside one of the other shacks and took it to use in our fire-pit and Roland left to do some snorkelling and fishing. I started to cook potatoes and our neighbours turned up in a white car so I went to have a chat about our surreal surroundings. They explained they were backpackers, one of was from France and the other was from Japan, they had met whilst working at an oyster farm. The second French guy answered their Gumtree add for a travel partner and they'd travelled from Broome. They were heading to Perth and heard about this campsite from another backpacker and had been there for three days.

    I returned to finish the cooking going on Roland's past results, I didn't have high hopes Roland would return with a fish so when he turned up empty handed it was as expected. At the beach we watched the sunset behind the clouds. It was a lovely' cozy' spot but very windy so we returned to the shelter of the shack. It took ages for Roland to get the fire going. The wind kept blowing it out and he had to rearrange the rocks in a complete circle so there was a bit of wind protection. Della sat on my lap to warm me but the cold wind sent me to the tent early.

In the morning after breakfast, we watched our neighbours pack their tents and head off. It was chilly but we dressed and drove to the blowholes for a look. Della and I didn't walk all the way down to the blowholes because there were plaques containing dates of the deaths of people who had been killed by king waves. Roland took the chance and went down but he returned in one piece. We drove on to the shipwreck memorial and read its plaque but it was too windy to stay long. Roland wanted to visit the station store to buy some fishing bait but when we arrived at the station they had a 'closed' store sign displayed at the entrance of the road that led to their houses. On the dirt road back to the station we passed a dead rotting sheep. If I were a farmer I wouldn't want people on my land, hitting my sheep with their vehicles. I would put out large 'No Trespassing' signs and lock gates at the entrance to keep my animals safe from reckless drivers.

Back at the camp, I decided to stay at the shack whilst Roland went fishing and snorkelling. When he returned he made pasta and sauce but he used too much salt and it was a very salty pasta dish. Roland walked down to the beach to watch the sunset behind clouds again and invited Della but she wanted to stay with me while I made apple pie for desert. The fire was easier to start that night as, by then, Roland learned the tricks of starting a fire in the wind. It was a large glowing fire that sent out sparks everywhere. In the morning, we packed and headed for Carnarvon. The music on Roland's USB stick was driving me insane, I couldn't stand his Beatles or jazz piano music anymore. Then I found he had music by the Red Hot Chili Peppers and I made him play it. He only let me play three Red Hot Chili Peppers songs before he was complaining he didn't like the music - *too loud and crazy*. We settled on Jamaraqui, but even a few days of Jamaqui, playing the entire time, was making me sick. I wanted to have a go searching that USB stick I was sure there was more fantastic music on it then he was letting on but Roland always had to be in charge of the USB stick and didn't like me pressing any buttons on the radio. We passed a large satellite dish and an even larger fake banana while driving into town and spying Jolly's Tire Service, pulled in. I explained that we had the tire fixed in Port Headland but were still having to inflate it every morning. I wondered if, having found one hole, the workman never bothered to look for a second leak. We were told they could fix it right away and to pull the car into the garage and they were happy to have Della left in the car.

Roland and I crossed the street to Woolies to shop and I bought Della a bag of dry dog food and some cans. I noticed the Christmas goodies for sale and heard the Christmas music playing. I thought to myself *I wonder where we'll be for Christmas*. We returned and paid $40.00 to fix the tire the headed to a riverside park for brunch. It was so yummy to have fresh salad and Turkish bread. We spent the next few hours at the beach and went for a swim in the shallow waters. After showers we drove to the One Mile Jetty and Roland sorted out his fishing gear and took Della fishing. The caretaker of the jetty came over for a chat carrying a glass of wine and I think it must have been her fourth glass. She was definitely ready to party and I found her very entertaining. After she left, I walked around the museum and read about the old train line and other old things that had been brought there from nearby stations. Roland returned with Della and three fish, (*finally!!*) two bream and another unknown fish. He said Della had been keen on fishing until she found the bait wasn't for her to eat, and then she'd lost interest and fell asleep on the blanket.

We drove to a nearby waterfront park and it had a barbie where Roland cooked the fish on one side of the grill and I grilled the potatoes, carrots, and onions on the other side. The vegetables were lovely, Roland ate the fish and Della ate the fish- tails and heads. It grew dark and we stopped at a drive-in bottle shop for Roland to buy a beer. A drunk Aboriginal man inside was giving the young blonde girl behind the counter a hard time. She was refusing service and a local man helped escort the man out as he was starting to get violent and yelling abuse at her. It took Roland more than ten minutes to buy the beer. Della and I sat in the car watching the whole scene play out. We left and stopped at the petrol station, but perhaps the attendant had experienced similar problems as he wouldn't open the door to give us the hose to check our tire pressure.

We drove south, stopped at a rest area and slept in the back of the car arriving at Shark Bay. After parking, we walked the boardwalk to view the Hamelin Pool stromatolites. Roland was quite excited about these, as he had read about them in Germany. Della ran around the boardwalk and I read all the information boards posted along the walk. There were small fish swimming between the stromatolites and we took a few pictures then left, driving to the caravan park shop. There we used the picnic table shelter to have our lunch and Della got into trouble by the park attendant for wandering around. I had to call Della back and tell her to stay close to me. The man behind the shop counter gave me a map of the area, suggesting things for us to do. We first stopped at Nanga beach and had a lovely swim in the shallow warm waters but Della didn't like the waves. The wind blew fiercely making us very cold when we exited the water. Looking for a more sheltered place, we found Shell Beach. Della stayed with the car as the sign said she wasn't allowed. I tied her up outside of the car and she crawled underneath the car enjoying the shade the car provided.

Shell beach was amazing instead of sand, the beach consisted entirely of small shells. We took a few pictures and looked at names in the sand made by people with the shells. Roland was inspired and said he wanted to write a love message in the 'shell sand' for his girlfriend, take a picture and send it to her. He said they were on a break while he was in Australia and he could have sex with whomever he wanted and she could see whomever she wanted. I asked what happened if, when he returned, she had another guy? He said it would be his loss. I felt a little weird about this situation, so I returned to the car while he wrote his love message to his girlfriend and wasn't too keen on Roland after this. We'd spent so much time together but I realised that I didn't really know this good-looking German after all. He returned and we drove to Denham Visitors' Centre to register to camp at Eagle Bluff but once again it was closed so we couldn't register. At the post I asked what time they fed the dolphins at Monkey Mia and was told 8am was the earliest. At the town beach we had showers then drove four kilometers down a dirt road to Eagle Bluff to set up the tent. It's located on top of a mountain-cliff that plunges straight down to the ocean. Wild dog poison baits signs were everywhere so poor Della had to be on the lead again. Eagle Bluff had a spectacular view and campsite but the problems presented themselves as soon as we tried to set up the tent. The wind never let up, consistently blowing hard and strong and it took both of us to hold on. The wind kept picking it up and whipping all over. If we didn't have a hold of something the wind picked it up and over the cliff in seconds. Roland put the mattress in the tent that helped hold it down then buried the corners and borders in sand to try to stop the tent from blowing over. That helped a bit, but the wind still shook all four sides of the tent. The wind caused the temperature to drop and I felt this was the windiest place I'd ever visited. My hair was in knots and I thought no wonder you have to register to use the campsite, they want to know when they should start looking for bodies and vehicles after they get blown off the cliff. Della hid under the car on her blanket. Roland and I retreated to the tent. I was hoping the tent would block the wind but it still rocked and I worried the wind might just rip the tent apart. The sun was starting to set, so Roland suggested a climb up the cliff to the top to watch the sunset. I wasn't real keen but he talked me into it. We climbed up the cliff to the boardwalk and it was a spectacular view of the sun dipping behind clouds on the horizon. We decided to walk the boardwalk the following day as it was getting late and we hadn't brought a flashlight. Della wanted to run all over during the walk but I kept her near me because I was afraid she would go sniffing out something poisonous. Back at the campsite Della went on the leash and slept on her blanket. Roland stayed outside to have a smoke but I climbed into the tent. Its walls were blowing about madly and I didn't think I would ever be able to fall asleep but I was tired and it only took a few minutes.

In the morning, we quickly packed and headed to the Denham Beach park to have our breakfast. It was less windy there and the picnic table shelter had brick walls that blocked the strong winds. We continued on to Monkey Mia and arrived there by 8am. Roland paid the entry fee and we walked down to the beach with Della on her lead. A female dolphin and baby dolphin swam around and no-one was allowed into the water because of the baby dolphin. An employee came down and fed the adult dolphin and then both dolphins swam out to sea. We waited for some hours hoping to see more dolphins as we were told that there are usually three dolphin-feedings a day before noon but no dolphins appeared so we spent the time watching documentaries about dolphins and the Shark Bay area.

Della and I walked down the street and I took photos of a building made completely from shells before returning to Eagle Bluff, where the wind was still blowing, and walked the boardwalk. It was a great view of the island and we could see sharks in the clear calm waters below. I spotted a lizard but didn't let Della chase it. She was so keen to have a chase but there were tourists taking pictures of it. Della was very well behaved and just watched the lizard run around I didn't even have to grab her collar to hold her back and obeyed my command.

Heading south, we were pulling into Geraldton, when Baz phoned from Roma. He told me he had a mate in Geraldton named Andy and gave me his phone number. I phoned Andy who was very nice on the phone and invited us to stay but explained he had just moved into a new place. He gave me the street address and we followed his directions, arriving at a small housing duplex. Andy's unit was located at the entrance, so we parked in the visitors' parking across from his unit. Andy answered the door, and I introduced us. He invited us in and Della went out back to visit Buster, Andy's large black dog. Della didn't really want to socialise with another dog, but she wasn't allowed in the house. Buster wanted to play, but Della kept ignoring him and would turn away from his efforts. Poor Buster had a girl at his place and she didn't want to play. Della is acting like me! Poor Roland had a girl in his land cruiser and she didn't want to play either. Andy agreed we could use his kitchen to cook and he accepted our invitation to join us for the meal. Whilst Roland organised the land cruiser and made the bed outside, Andy offered me a cider while I cooked and we shared stories of how we met Baz. Andy explained that he'd met him in a bar when Baz was trying to sell gold nuggets there. Andy decided to shout Baz a beer and that is how they met.

While eating tea in the lounge room, Andy told us some fantastic tales. We swapped a few stories about our lives and he appeared to be a very interesting and intriguing individual, having had wild and exciting times. Andy also let it slip that he'd started work at 3am that day, driving a local delivery truck, so I kept that in mind and made sure we didn't keep him up too late.

We went to our bed in the car and Della stayed with Buster in the backyard. Later in the land cruiser, Roland made the comment that, compared to Andy and me, his life was boring and to date, his biggest life adventure was this trip the year travelling around Australia. I told him some people are content and happy with having a home, vehicle and a job, but then when they talk to adventurous individuals like Andy and I they start to think maybe they have missed out 'it's makes you happy'. Roland said he was very happy living in Germany and working full-time in a factory. I revealed my time working in a factory had lasted one day - the job had been so repetitive and boring I didn't go back the next. Roland replied he thought factory life was the best and said if everyone was like me, there would be no- one working in factories. My answer was that's why it's so good that everyone is different all the jobs in the world got done by people who love their work. I told Roland he needed to realise that 'you can make your life exciting if you want to. It's your choice to seize the moment and see where it takes you.'

Next morning I went into Andy's unit, took a shower and made us breakfast. I thanked Andy for letting us stay and making us feel so welcome. We said our goodbyes and headed off to the public library. When we arrived there the sign said it opened at 1:30pm, so we walked to the beach with Della. We came across a Visitors' Centre and I went inside and picked up a map of the area. Roland was keen to do sand surfing that was advertised in one of the brochures. I wasn't so keen as I had just taken a shower and was feeling lovely and clean. We came across a Backpackers' Hostel and I went inside to enquire about the Internet. I met a gorgeous girl from Holland who explained the best free place was the library. So I walked back down-stairs and she followed me with a Japanese and an Australian backpacker. She overheard Roland and my conversation regarding the sand surfing beach and invited me to join their group to go to the local museum. It was free entry, so I agreed. Roland didn't want to go but we agreed to meet at the library at 1:30pm. I left with Della and the group of backpackers walking to the museum. And Roland went to his land cruiser and drove off. After so long with Roland, it was nice chatting to new people.

Leaving Della tied up outside, the museum was interesting and very informative about the local area. I especially liked the shipwrecked stories, the tales and relics of ships that sunk on the rugged Australian shoreline. When I left there, Della and I walked around town and visited a few parks and she enjoyed running around after the sticks I threw.

I stopped at a local art gallery and looked at the pictures and interesting pieces made from recycled products. They had a dress for sale made completely from the tabs off aluminium cans but the price on the dress was over $2,000. I headed to the library and Della waited outside while I went inside to use the computer. Roland arrived and used his laptop in the library and we spent a few hours there with me regularly leaving the library to check on Della. We decided to head to the Ellensdale Pool and stay the night there, stopped to take snap-shots at the leaning trees and the wind farm on the way. I noticed that Della had started to pose for the camera and took a great photo of her in front of the gorgeous Ellensdale Pool. This was a lovely non-windy campsite and we slept in the back of the land-cruiser.

The next morning we took a swim in the lovely refreshing pool Della swam after sticks that I threw in the water for her, she just loved swimming after them but when she brought the sticks to shore she chewed them up into little pieces. We left Ellensdale pool around 10am and I drove south for a while and stopped to shop in Jurien Bay, where we had a picnic lunch on the green grassy beachside park. It was a nice spot with but the best part was eating fresh salad vegetables on toasted rye bread. It was wonderful fresh food and I ate three salad sandwiches. We headed off to Cervantes and stopped at the Visitors' Information Office to obtain a local map. Back at the car Roland offered to take Della with him and go fishing so I stayed and wrote my diary. Whilst I was writing, a black sedan pulled up beside Roland's car. It contained two Japanese males in the front seat and three Japanese ladies in the back. One of the male passengers rolled down his window and asked directions to the local Stromatolites. I started giving directions, but he couldn't understand my English so I walked to the driver's door and gave the driver the street to enter into their GPS, but he couldn't figure it either. I sighed, and reached through the window entering the town and street name myself. They thanked me and drove off with me wondering how they had managed to get to that little town.

Della returned from fishing, I guess she got tired of seeing the fish eat the bait. After I fed Della her dinner, I took her to the beach and threw sticks in the ocean she swam out and retrieved them to chew up. We walked down the jetty to check on Roland and there was a little boy with pots trying to catch crabs. Roland said he'd caught two fish, he showed me the photos but he'd released them because he didn't want to kill them and eat them. (*I must be rubbing off on him!*). Roland packed his fishing gear; we headed down the jetty to the car, and drove towards The Pinnacles and Kangaroo Point. It was located in the National park and it had 'no camping' and 'no dogs' signs all everywhere. We quickly abandoned that location and drove down a dirt road, past the jetty to be met by signs saying 'no camping' but we found a sandy road that led to the beach and parked in the scrub.

Chapter Eleven

Homeward Bound

Della's barking woke me up. A vehicle drove past on the sandy dirt track. I was worried that someone would come out and fine us for parking there so I pretty much dragged Roland out of the back of the vehicle and drove to a rest area.

I closed the curtains in the back and put our supplies in the middle so Della would have to sit in the back. I didn't want to take any chances with a park ranger seeing her and giving us a fine, we headed for The Pinnacles. Roland enjoyed them, and took lots of pictures but I mostly stayed in the car - I didn't want to leave Della. I left the car only twice to have Roland take a picture. Della couldn't even look out… I caught her sticking her head under the back curtain to see out the window and had to crawl in and safety pin the curtain whilst explaining that she wasn't allowed to look, because the ranger might see her. Poor Della she just wanted to have a 'sticky beak'. She was so good and didn't try to look out anymore…just looked in the windshield from the back of the land cruiser. We were stopped on the way out by the park ranger, but the ranger just wanted Roland to pay the entrance fee, since Roland had failed to put money into the Honesty Box. Della stayed silently in the back of the land cruiser as Roland paid the $11 entrance fee and we drove off.

We headed south towards Perth and stopped at a rest area on the river. It was a shallow stream with a sandy bottom and had clear running water and Della jumped in straight away. I climbed the embankment to the car and changed into my swimsuit - my black sports bra and knickers that I used for bathers - I collected my soap, razor and towel and Roland changed into his boardies. We went down to the river and I took my bath whilst Roland just waded in saying he wanted to take a shower. Later, at the car, I soaked my feet in warm water I'd heated up and used the foot soak scrub from my package that Yasmin had mailed to me. It felt wonderful to have clean exfoliated feet again. It made me happy, but my mood wasn't shared by Roland. He was worried about not finding a job when we arrived in Perth and having to live in his car - the city police could give him a fine for sleeping in his car.

We drove on towards Perth and Roland directed me to a northern coastal suburb in Perth. We drove to the beach park and Roland took a shower – he complained that the water temperature was colder than the river, the main reason I opted for the river bath, rather than wait for a shower. The Gumtree French boys phoned me to say they had read my email and had a free seat in their car. I asked them to text me their hostel name and address and I would meet them later in the day. I couldn't understand the French accent whilst talking on my mobile and didn't know where they were staying.

After Roland finished his shower, I had a hot coffee waiting for him to warm him up. We headed to the main library and drove around trying to find a free car park.

The city of Perth had no free car parks downtown, so we parked in the garage under the library, leaving Della in the car with the windows down and we went up in the elevators to the library. On Gumtree I looked for the French boys ad. I was going to email them and ask for the hostel name and address, since I hadn't received their information (perhaps they didn't understand my question). Instead I found Alexandria's ad... she was now in Perth looking for a person to go to Byron Bay, New South Wales. So I emailed her but also found an ad from Toomas offering a free lift to Adelaide.

I called Toomas and found his Estonian English much better than the French guys' English. Toomas explained that he'd checked out of his hostel that morning and was driving around Perth waiting to leave the city at night. I asked Toomas to text me a location where we could meet in about thirty minutes. I went back inside the library and helped Roland finish his letter to a potential employer and we returned to the car. I entered a street name into the GPS and we soon showed up at a McDonalds. Toomas was waiting in the parking lot next to his white land cruiser. I jumped out and introduced myself then Della jumped out and I introduced her. Toomas seemed friendly, ready to go and had no worries with either of us so Roland and I began unloading his vehicle of my supplies that were scattered everywhere. I started shoving things into my bags and hoping I didn't forget anything. Roland remembered my bathers hanging from the curtains and, at the last minute, I remembered my towel hanging up. Roland kept saying that this was too sudden but, hidden from Toomas's view, I just kissed his neck, hugged him tight and said my sad goodbye.I could tell he was sad to see me go and I was sad too, but I couldn't pass up a free lift.

Della hopped into Toomas's car like she had been doing it the whole time. I saw Roland give Della a good pat through the open window and, as I sat down, started missing Roland. I blew him a kiss good-bye and he returned it. As we pulled away, I was wondering if I'd done the right thing, leaving Roland like that…it'd happened so fast. Out of the window I saw Roland sitting in his driver's seat, glumly watching us leave. I looked back knowing I would miss him.

Toomas's land cruiser had no air or music - for a moment I wondered why, in three States, I seemed unable to find a ride that had air-conditioning - at *least the seats*

Toomas and Della

are comfortable, I thought. In the back, Della sat on a mattress with her own window - opened for her viewing and sniffing pleasure. This was the best ride for her so far...no wonder she'd jumped right in as soon as she saw the plush mattress.

Toomas explained he and his brother had flown to Perth from Estonia. Apparently there is a large group of Estonians that live and work in Perth. Some have two year visas, some don't bother and just stay when they fly home they are banned from returning to Australia for two years. Some Estonians have been living and working in Perth for years and never planning on returning home. Toomas had been staying in a double room with his brother at the Perth hostel. Toomas had paid his half ($230.00 a week) in rent and had been in the construction industry, building concrete walls for houses. He wanted to get a two-year visa, so he was traveling to Adelaide for work. If he was able to work for three months in a small town then he'd be granted another year on his visa. When I queried this he explained that Adelaide was considered a 'small town' by the Australian Government.

I soon found Hungry Jacks and McDonald's were Toomas's favourite places to eat. Every time I offered food, during our time traveling together, he declined. Instead he ate at the roadhouses or fast food outlets. We had left Roland around 4pm and we'd made it just west of Kangorilee before we stopped for the night. I kept falling asleep while Toomas was driving…. I felt bad. I should have been awake talking to him. We pulled behind a building next to the city park and slept in the back on the mattress. I helped Toomas put his sheets on the mattress and placed all our gear on the front seats. Della slept under the car and did her warning bark in the morning when someone walked past the vehicle.

I pulled the sheets to one side of the mattress and stacked our stuff on top of the folded sheet. I didn't want Della to get her hair all over Toomas's clean white sheets.

Next morning, we headed off and stopped to ask for a map at the Visitors Information Centre. We had been using Toomas's iPhone, but the screen was too small to properly see where we were heading. Toomas received directions to the nearest MacDonald's so he could have breakfast whilst I collected a road maps all the way to Adelaide. After Toomas's breakfast, we stopped at the Super Pit and took pictures of the huge hole in the earth created by gold miners. It was an amazing sight to see how deep humans can dig earth… the hole looked like it went all the way through to the other side of the world.

While returning to the vehicle, Della wanted to have a run around and play, but there were no sticks for me to throw, only rocks. We stopped off at the petrol station and Toomas filled up with petrol. The first tank held unleaded petrol, the second tank held LPG Autogas. As soon as I saw the showers behind the roadhouse, I headed there. In that wonderful shower, I washed my hair and my underwear and on the way to the car, I found a two-dollar coin on the ground. Clean and refreshed, I felt this was my lucky day!

For the next few hours I read about the interesting spots we could stop at along the route we were taking. The first red dot on the map was the city of Norseman. We stopped there to put more petrol in the land-cruiser and Toomas wanted lunch. We checked all over that tiny, partially-abandoned town for a McDonalds but Toomas had to settle for a cafe.

Back on the road, our next red dot was Eucalyptus Trees. There were many tall majestic trees but we didn't stop – just admired them and drove past. Della enjoyed sticking her head out her own window and looking and sniffing but I think she enjoyed sleeping on the mattress even more. For both of us, this was our first time driving across the Nullarbor Plain, and we had been expecting heaps of sand and nothing else. It was a pleasant surprise to find it wasn't desert. There were trees, shrubs, grasses, wildlife, and hills but, as I'd been warned, the Nullarbor really is boring to drive across. It's a very long straight road with no signs of people inhabiting the area, just endless plains - but they were full of nature and life.

Our next red map dot was the Balladonia Cultural Heritage Museum. I wanted to stop to see the history of the Afghan cameleers but Toomas wasn't keen. I managed to convince him by mentioning the NASA Skylab crashed spaceship was located in the museum. We pulled into the roadhouse and found the museum was attached to the petrol station.

As we alighted from the vehicle, we realised we would have to walk through the petrol station, then the souvenir shop, to get to the free museum. There was a sign that dogs weren't allowed in the museum so I left Della tied up in the shade, outside the shop. The museum was small but only slightly interesting. It had a huge stuffed camel toy with a story about cameleers and a piece of the spaceship that was retrieved from the nearby area.

Although our next red map dot was the Caiguna Blowhole, when we arrived at the Caiguna roadhouse we realised we had passed the turnoff to view the Blowhole. I showed Toomas the pictures of the blowhole I had taken near Carnarvon, but he wasn't impressed so we didn't turn drive back. We continued east onto the Eyre Highway. Out of the blue, after acres of nothing, we came across a large sign with a vehicle pulled in front of it…and a person taking pictures. We quickly realised that this must be the 'Australia's Longest Straight Road' sign. As it was on our map of 'things to see on the Nullarbor ', we stopped and waited for the tourists to take their snaps and then took our own touristy photos.

The tall trees were gone…now we were passing shrub and scrubby grass-covered land. We pulled off the Highway at the Madura Pass and went down the dirt track. Tiny wallabies exploded out of the bush, jumping all over the road. Della was beside herself with excitement. I asked Toomas to stop the land cruiser and told Della that she could chase them, expecting Della to wait till I opened the door so she could get out, but she was so happy she took a flying leap out the window and she was off running. All the wallabies jumped over a fence and just sat there looking back at her. Della ran up and down the length of the fence looking for a way in. I was a bit concerned for the wallabies. They just sat there staring back – they seemed to be laughing at her. Della can be very determined and I was sure she would find a hole and squeeze her way into that paddock but the wallabies knew that fence better than we did and their confidence wasn't misplaced. Eventually the wallabies became bored watching Della. They hopped up and down the fence-line to give Della a reason to keep trying to get them until they saw Della starting to size up the height of the fence to jump over it. The wallabies appeared to decide that teasing Della might not be in their best interest. They headed for the back of the paddock and were soon out of sight. So I called Della back to the car and we drove to the lookout where Toomas took scenic photos from the roof of the land cruiser.

That night, at the border of West Australia and South Australian, we passed the first quarantine checkpoint border and it was closed. We stopped at a rest area soon after and had a sleep in the back of the car. We were within viewing distance of the ocean and the area was windy so Della slept inside, in the front of the car. In the morning, I went to use the bush toilet, as there were no restrooms. Behind the bushes was smelly, filthy, and disgusting. Everyone had gone to the toilet behind those bushes…it reeked of urine and was littered with toilet paper. I thought *the government really needs to install toilets there.*

We continued and stopped at the Nullarbor Roadhouse. Toomas filled up the land cruiser with Autogas and bought breakfast, while Della and I filled up the water bottles and took pictures of the 'animal crossing' road sign and the killer whale statue. We passed the second quarantine checkpoint and this one was open. We pulled up to the 'stop' sign and an officer, walking to put some trash in the bin, saw us and wandered over. He asked us if we had fruit or vegetables and we replied that we hadn't. He said he had to search anyways so I got out and threw away the trash bag and Toomas opened the back door for him to search but he wasn't very thorough and let us through. We didn't have anything anyway, but he could have looked behind the front seats and in the glove-box like the Northern Territory quarantine checkpoint had.

We stopped off at Ceduna to obtain information about the ferry to Adelaide and to have a shower. When we visited the Visitors Information Centre first, the guy behind the desk was the most unhelpful person I've encountered on the whole trip and I was very tempted to write a letter of complaint. We asked about the ferry and he handed us a brochure. The brochure had no prices, so we asked him how much the ferry costs? He said to call the number or look on the website. We left and drove to the library to use the computer to look at the ferry website but the library was closed so we returned to the Information Centre and asked if we could use his computer to look. He allowed this but in reality he should have done this in the first place and should have known the ferry prices.

When we discovered it was half price fares for two days we were keen but told we had to pre book on the phone. We left the Centre to call and discovered that Toomas had no reception on his mobile. As I had no credit on my mobile, we went back in and explained this to the useless person behind the counter. He told us to go use a pay phone. We explained that we weren't from the area (obviously) and didn't know where the pay phones were located. He told us the shopping centre and post office had phones.

We walked to the shopping centre and tried to use the pay phone but it kept rejecting our coins. We walked to the post office and didn't see any phones so inside I asked the friendly post clerk. He explained that the phone booths were located behind the shop. Finally, we found them round the back and ended up using $3.00 in coins to make a 60 cent call for the ferry booking. The phone kept dropping out and we had to put more coins in and redial. As we left the phones, I thought, that the guy at the Visitors Information Center had no customers and should have offered to call or let us use his landline to make the ferry booking. The Ceduna Visitors Centre must be the worst information Centre in Australia. At other visitors centres I've visited in Australia, they go 'above and beyond' to help. At the Roebourne Visitors Centre, they actually called the library and found the library opening times for Roland and I so we could use the Internet and even drew us a map to get there.

We continued on our way, stopping off in the small towns we passed and Toomas filled up with Autogas as it was cheaper to drive on. We stopped at a rest area in Cleve, and the town looked empty...there was no one was around so I used the ladies restroom sink as my shower. Della laid down by the door and I used her collapsible bowl. I filled up the bowl with water from the sink and dump it over me. Then I soaped up and rinsed off with more bowls of water dumped over me. The water flowed into the drain in the middle of the restroom and I felt refreshed after our long day in the heat.

We headed for Cowell and found a '*no camping*' sign next to a pub but we parked there anyway. It was too early for us to sleep, so we headed to the pub for a drink. The bartender said they were closed but that the pub down the street was opened. So we ran to the pub before it shut. We arrived and, for a little country town it was pumping. The pub had seven very drunk blokes singing to the music playing on the jukebox, playing billiards, and dropping drinks on the floor. We sat at the bar, had two drinks apiece and got out of there fast, back to the land cruiser. I put Della in the front seat to sleep and Toomas and I slept in the back on the mattress. In the morning, I played with Della by throwing sticks while Toomas walked around looking for breakfast.

We arrived at Lucky Bay over an hour earlier than we needed to. Della went for a swim and Toomas bought the ferry tickets. He drove onto the ferry and parked. The land cruiser had no parking brake, so Toomas was worried the whole trip that his car would roll into the vehicle behind or the one in front. Della had to stay in the car the whole trip and I walked around seeking anyone travelling to Queensland but no one was going that way.

It was a pleasant trip to Wallaroo, South Australia even the kids on the ferry weren't too annoying. I had only wanted to tell them to behave once, but I refrained and instead told the little girl, that if the glass floor she was standing on broke, she would fall into the ocean and the killer sharks would eat her, because sharks loved eating children. She said that sounded scary and the two kids ran off to stay with their parents and left us in peace.

When we were allowed back to our vehicles, we discovered that Della had been sea-sick. We drove off the ferry, and stopped at a beach rest area next to the jetty. I cleaned out the back of the car, and washed the mattress and sheets, while Della ran around and drank water. Toomas was very understanding and wasn't upset at all. I was terribly relieved as some people would have thrown a fit. We stopped at the Kadina library to use the free Internet and I checked Gumtree. I found a bloke going our way and he was leaving that afternoon. Scott's mobile was switched off and looking at the time, I figured he'd already left. Alexandria was leaving Adelaide on the 26th of Dec and had an empty car. The people she'd been traveling with were staying in Adelaide so I emailed her too. We headed off again and continued our drive to Adelaide. I tried Scott one more time on Toomas's phone but there no answer so I sent a text message and left it at that.

We arrived in Adelaide and I directed Toomas to some hostels but they wanted too much money but he was told of a hostel not on the map. We drove there and he decided to stay.

Scott returned my call on Toomas's mobile and I learned he was a local Adelaide guy, driving to visit his cousin on Bribie Island. Scott said he'd wanted to leave that afternoon but hadn't finished packing however he would be able to leave the next day, if I was still interested. I agreed and we arranged for Scott to pick up Della and I at 4pm from the hostel. Toomas parked his car in the hostel car park and checked in and arranged to meet again at 8pm. Della and I walked to the park and she ran around chasing sticks and having fun. Back at the car park, I gathered together my shower stuff and followed Toomas into the hostel. I took a shower and returned to the land cruiser to sleep in the back with Della. I had no money for the hostel and I didn't want to leave Della.

In the morning, Della and I climbed out of the back of the land cruiser and heard a backpacker telling housekeeping staff I had slept in the back of the car. Quickly, I packed, locked up the car and Della and I went to the park. We walked around the city in the parks all morning till we came to the library and went inside to use the Internet, leaving Della to rest in the shade.

Later we spend time in the park and Della went swimming in the lake before walking back to Toomas's car and retrieved my shower stuff, deciding not to use the hostel shower as they might be watching out for me. I walked to the public toilets and found it was one of those annoying music-playing, automatic ones. Della and I went inside and I pushed the button to close and lock the door. I knew I only had ten minutes to take a shower and my time had started. Quickly I stripped and filled up the water bottle from the automatic sink and dumped water over me twice, soaped up and then rinsed off with a few more water-filled bottles. I put my contacts in and then the warning sound started. I dressed as fast and the door automatically opened slowly as I pulled up my shorts.

The very loud and annoying alarm sounded. I felt like I'd been caught robbing a bank! Della and I ran out of the toilet and went behind the stall so I could finish putting my dirty clothes and shower stuff in my bag and apply sunscreen. The alarm kept sounding and people were staring and I felt guilty - like I had committed a crime. Della and I got out of there as soon as I got my stuff together. The alarm was still sounding off when we left. I don't know who resets these alarms but it's very loud and embarrassing. It lets everyone know that you have been in the toilet for ten minutes. What if I was having a bowel problem and it took more than ten minutes? The door would open, the alarm would sound and alert everyone to look at you sitting on the toilet. Bloody hell, who thought that up?

We walked back to the hostel car park and collected my stuff putting it in a pile on the pavement. I just started to organise it when Scott pulled up in his black SUV - with no air conditioning. (Of course!) He was surprised to see Della but took it in his stride. We made room for Della on the back seat and put my gear in the back. Scott had short black hair and used to be a mechanic. He wasn't working as he'd been a passenger in a car that had rolled over a few times and he'd ended up in hospital. He was going to spend the holidays with his cousin and her three kids on Bribie Island as his mother was annoying him a bit too much. Scott loved his mum but sometimes she became too interested in his affairs. He said his mum had spent too much time talking to his mates on Facebook. Scott had rock CD's and an IPAD and liked the same music as me, so that was great.

Scott and Della

With Della sticking her head out the window, we drove through some beautiful vineyards and started to look for a place to camp. We pulled off onto a dirt road as a million rabbits exploded out of everywhere! Della was so excited, I reached over and grabbed her collar and held on, afraid she would jump out the window and run after them. We slowly drove down the road with rabbits running and jumping everywhere. We pulled up next to a quiet peaceful lake and stopped. Della was gone as soon as her door opened. Scott pointed out a 'no camping' sign, so we couldn't stay there. I decided to take a quick swim while Della chased the rabbits- she was having so much fun. With so many rabbits, she couldn't choose just one to chase - it was funny watching her running around in circles. I stepped into the sandy bottom lake and looked up at the full moon and thought of Roland and how he would have loved to be in this 'cozy' spot. Roland and his' cozy' spots…he definitely would have called this 'cozy'. It was a lovely swim as it was a warm evening and I dressed, feeling refreshed. I blew the whistle, Della jumped into the backseat and we headed off to find a camping spot.

Scott had informed me he had driven this route many times and he knew there would be a spot by the river coming up soon. Sure enough, he soon found us a place by the river and well off the highway…Della could run around all night and not be on a leash. We set up our swags and had a great chat. I found that Scott had led a very interesting life - almost as exciting as Andy from Geraldton.

It was good to sleep in my swag again, I had missed it. In the morning, there was Della in my face as soon as I unzipped the swag. She tries to lick my face when I get up and I grab her collar and hold her away at arms' length, till I wake up enough to find a stick for her to chase. I'm not a 'coz'y person in the morning, as Roland would say. I headed to the river with Della for a swim and we swam for a while as the temperature was already heating up.

The temperature hit 42 Celsius that day and we stopped off at another lake to have a swim and cool down. There were a few local blokes and dogs putting their wave runners and boats in the lake. This lake had a sandy bottom and was icy cold and I took a long swim out and back. Della just tried to stay away from the two large dogs that wanted to play with her. She swam out to me and they swam after her so she swam for shore and hid under Scott's car. The dogs were too big to climb under the car and soon forgot her…Della can be quite unsocial with other dogs. We said goodbye to the dogs and continued on down the road. We stopped at a store and Scott bought a beer and a vodka ice-cruiser for me. I drank my cold drink but then drifted off to sleep. When I woke up, it was still hot and I reapplied sunscreen. We stopped off at a pub in a small town and I couldn't be bothered with putting shorts on and I walked into the pub wearing my singlet and underwear. The overweight old lady behind the bar gave me the evil eye but all the customers perked right up – including her husband, the bartender. I sat at the bar and Scott sat next to me and ordered a beer and I ordered a glass of iced water… I didn't want another drink as it made me sleepy in the heat. It was lovely and cool inside the bar, Della waited for us outside by the bar door in the shade, so she got a cool breeze every time the door was opened and she could see me. I drank two glasses of iced water and then we said our goodbyes. A local man said we could use his sprinkler next door to hose Della and help cool her off. Thanking him, I picked up the sprinkler and cooled Della off before we continued driving.

Every time we stopped at a petrol station Della and I would go to the restrooms and fill up our water bottles.

Scott stopped at the Hay Visitor Centre where there were free showers and we each had a cold shower before driving on. We stopped at the entrance to a few towns and had our photos taken in front of the welcome sign. We passed Dubbo and our next camp spot was on the side of the highway as couldn't find another nearby site. Della had to be on the leash overnight but the rest area had toilets and picnic shelters. I set up my swag under the shelter and Scott set up his bed on the table. It looked like it was going to rain and we sat on the table watching the lightning show in the distance. It was pretty spectacular, and the steady flashing went on for over an hour, lightning up the whole sky. We headed off early before the heat started setting in stopping off in Tamworth and Scott bought a few drinks and a bag of ice for the esky.

I drove to a rest stop on top of a mountain that overlooked Tamworth. It was a lovely view and Della ran around chasing sticks. Scott took over the driving and, despite the temperature going as high as 32 Celsius, that day ended up being a pleasant driving day. We stopped at a 'driver reviver' in Thunderbolt and chatted to a lovely couple working there. They told us the 'Thunderbolt story'. He was a highway man who hid behind rocks and robbed rich people with a gun and gave the booty to the poor. He was the town's Robin Hood and escaped the law and dieing in Canada in the 1800's. The lady telling the story sounded like she would have been first in the queue to date Thunderbolt. We thanked them and headed off to the astoundingly beautiful waterfalls in the Guy Fawkes National Park we took pictures and soaked in the view.

The road to Grafton was just amazingly scenic. The simple narrow windy road went up and down the mountains; lovely tall forest trees, cool breezes, and very

Della and I at the Falls

loud crickets assaulted our senses - a perfect and gorgeous drive. Scott's vehicle had a digital temperature display and I saw it had cooled down to a pleasant 26 Celsius.

We drove all the way to Coraki and, when we pulled up to my place, it looked abandoned. The green long grass peeped over the fence and the gate wouldn't open so Scott used his pliers and made an entrance in the fence. Della and I walked up the driveway and Scott followed us in his car. I opened the roller door and, relieved, discovered my place intact. I walked into the shed and quickly became covered in spider-webs…I just swept them away from my face knowing that, if that happened five months ago, I would have been screaming by now. I continued until I reached the back door and tried to push it open – the long grass outside adding to the difficulty. Then I saw Lucky's blanket folded up. It was lying on the lounge chair and I remembered Lucky wasn't returning home. Lucky and Della had been in great shape and were built for a trip like this. I was unfit and figured I might get bitten by a snake, get sunstroke, or die of dehydration but our trip was over and Della and I were the only ones to return. I missed Lucky so much and I'd thought about him every day of the trip. I never got to swim with Lucky... every time I went into the water, I'd think *would Lucky go swimming with us this time or would he just stand by the shore and wait for us to return?* Some days were so hot I just knew Lucky would have gone swimming with us. When we walked past a patch of green grass, I would think *Lucky would've insisted on stopping and having a munch.* Lucky was a best mate who can never be replaced...a perfect horse and feel I never appreciated him the way I should have. I wish I'd given him more hugs, kisses, pats, and carrots. We learn from regrets, and I won't make that mistake again. Della receives lots of hugs, kisses, cuddles, and pats every single day.

The question, I ask myself is, if I had known Lucky would die on this trip, what would I have done? The answer is always the same; I would have stayed home and not had this adventure. Lucky was more important than any trip or adventure but then I think of some of the wonderful people I met along the way, Darren and Megan Lunow, Joe Green, Peggy and Jack Ferguson, Morris, Heidi, John Riley, Pat, Lorelle, Roland, Baz, Andy, and Scott.

I never would have realised how special Lucky was to me if I hadn't completed this trip. If we knew what the future held for us, there wouldn't be many adventures in this world. As Arthur Miller said – 'Maybe all one can do is hope to end up with the right regrets.

Our adventures will continue in *Della's Destiny: Murray River* and you can also follow Della's adventures on her Facebook Page: Della's Destiny.

Glossary

To do a "runner" – To take off with out hesitation.

Hobbles – a device that prevents the locomotion of horses legs by tethering them together.

Easy boots – a protective cover for a horse's hooves, work boots.

A Picket line – a horizontal rope, along which horses are tied at intervals.

Billy – a pot used to boil water.

Bloke – Man.

Bolted – another term for running away very fast without warning.

Cuppa – a cup of coffee, tea, or hot chocolate, a hot drink.

Chatted – to have a conversation with someone.

www.ingramcontent.com/pod-product-compliance
Ingram Content Group UK Ltd.
Pitfield, Milton Keynes, MK11 3LW, UK
UKHW021253180426
11947UKWH00010B/750